PROSPECTS FOR THE SOUL
Soundings in Jungian Psychology and Religion

PROSPECTS FOR THE SOUL

Soundings in Jungian Psychology and Religion

VERA VON DER HEYDT

DARTON, LONGMAN AND TODD

First published in Great Britain in 1976 by
Darton, Longman and Todd Ltd
85 Gloucester Road, London SW7 4SU

© Vera von der Heydt 1976

ISBN 0 232 51338 4

Printed in Great Britain by The Anchor Press Ltd
and bound by Wm Brendon & Son Ltd
both of Tiptree, Essex

FOR SANDRA

CONTENTS

Preface   ix

ASPECTS OF MAN   1

1. The Parent Archetype   2
2. On the Animus   12
3. Psychic Energy   23
4. Personal Enthusiasm   29
5. Loneliness   36

ANALYTICAL PSYCHOLOGY AND THE CHRISTIAN   43

6. Jung and Religion   44
7. Alchemy   57
8. Psychological Implications of the Dogma of the Assumption   70
9. The Treatment of Catholic Patients   77
10. An Approach to Prayer   86
11. Fear, Guilt and Confession   92

Epilogue   107

Bibliography   109

Willst du dich selber erkennen, so sieh, wie die andern es treiben,
Willst du die andern verstehen, blick in dein eigenes Herz.

(If you wish to know yourself, then look at the actions of others,
If you wish to understand others, then look into your own heart.)

Sayings, Friedrich von Schiller.

PREFACE

All the essays in this book are the outcome of my work as a Jungian analyst. I have been practising for just over thirty years, and during this time many changes have taken place in the outside world, as well as in attitudes to life. However, essentially people have not yet changed: there is still much fear and much loneliness; relationships have not become any easier, and the search for meaning and spiritual fulfilment continues. The great problem is still how to get to know oneself, how to relate to what one really is, and to recognise the conditionings and prejudices which keep one in a state of unconsciousness. No-one can do this completely alone – we all need help. A book may set us on our way, or a friend or a clergyman; even someone sitting in front of us on a bus may inadvertently make a helpful remark. We may join some kind of group and we may even find ourselves facing an analyst. There are many different ways in which we can become aware of our basic problem, and chance may well cast a glimmer of light on it. But the kind of inner conflict that tears us apart can only be resolved through careful and patient attention, and this is a long and hard task. We need another human being to encourage us to continue our searchings when we are in the wilderness.

Our response to indirect information or to answers to questions as yet unformulated is sometimes acceptance immediately followed by appropriate action. Sometimes, however, one is too identified with and unconscious of the nature of one's problem to be able to listen or to see the key which could open the door of one's prison. One resists by being inattentive or by proclaiming that no-one can help because things are too difficult or not sufficiently serious to warrant asking for help, or else one may believe that one is unworthy of assistance. All these attitudes indicate a state of ego inflation; one feels that one ought, should, must be strong enough to get over or through any difficulties unaided; to ask for help or to receive it would be an admission of weakness and failure. Sometimes people may even go so far as to accept help only to reject it as soon as possible in order to be in the position of projecting failure and weakness on to another, so keeping one's own sense of power, one's omnipotence intact. As I realised during my analysis, I myself was slow to react to hints and late in waking from unconscious identifications and conditionings.

I was born in Berlin at the turn of the century, and had an elder sister and a younger brother. My father was a merchant banker, a Jew who carried in himself a heritage of Eastern as well as of Western culture: Eastern German and Dutch. As a boy he had joined the Protestant Church because, as he explained to me one day, he believed that it was right for a citizen to belong to the official religion of his country. My father was an introvert, melancholic, and more interested in politics, music and philosophy than in banking. My mother was half Nordic, half Celtic: German and Irish. She was extrovert and sanguine, loved being with people and was interested in all things beautiful. She had been brought up as a Lutheran though her mother had been a lapsed Roman Catholic. Despite differences in cultural background and temperament, my parents were devoted to each other and in accord over important matters. Their ideas on education were very progressive; they believed that knowledge is essential for the enjoyment of life and that, if at all possible, a child's individual bent should be taken into account. At the age of twelve I was sent to a small school where girls were prepared for university; I took the course based on mathematics, physics and chemistry because, so my mother told me, it was vital for me to learn to think. My sister went to a conventional girls' school where, I gather, she was supposed to learn how to be more conventional!

My schooldays were a wonderful period; I felt happy and free with my companions and with my teachers. The headmaster was an outstanding person and always approachable. An incident which was of the greatest significance to me was when I asked to see him because I wanted to know whether he believed in the immortality of the soul. This was a question I would never have asked my parents. They knew only the outer world of reality: achievement and success in everything one did were not so much demanded as expected. They knew nothing of the reality of the inner world nor of the psyche. They were unaware that my inner inheritance – the conflicting strains within myself – was tearing me to pieces. I realised increasingly my racial and spiritual 'otherness'; I was different not only from my friends but from my family as well. My headmaster suggested that I read Plato and Moses Mendelssohn, and it was partly owing to his influence that I began reading the Mystics – Jewish, Christian and Indian. I became more and more aware of another dimension. In early childhood I had been very delicate, but during my years at school I no longer got seriously ill and therefore did not need to withdraw from overdemands or a too-harsh light of negative criticism. At home I was considered stupid – pretty, but stupid. The real point was that I had never been able to identify with any other member of my family. Neither of my parents was a romantic, searching for the 'blue flower' or for the inner centre.

When the first world war broke out I was fourteen. My parents were patriotic but never nationalistic, and it was mainly through their realistic appraisal of the situation and their despair that I experienced those tragic years. I was very split at that time, looking inwards for something I did not seem able to find, keeping the ideas which preoccupied me to myself, and conforming to the demands made on me by my environment. Towards the end of the war I met my future husband. He was much older, but I was drawn to him because he took me seriously and I could talk to him. He gave me books on Eastern systems of religious thought and art which were a revelation to me. We were married much sooner than we had expected – on Armistice Day but to the sound of machine guns, for it was also the first day of the revolution in Berlin. My husband had to return to his post at the German Legation in The Hague, and the reason my parents had favoured the precipitate marriage was to get at least one of their children to safety. I felt very guilty at leaving my family to an uncertain future, but I gave in to their pressure and to my husband's pleadings. (Some years later I found myself in a similar situation; I felt even more guilty, but I knew then that I had to leave Germany.) There were many happy times in my married life, but also many difficult ones, and in the end I returned to my parents. I still continued to live in a curious state of unconsciousness, a kind of vacuum. My divorce shook me badly and I gradually woke up to the realisation that the something I had been looking for within myself was an inner power pushing me out of a collective, conditioned environment into shaping my own life.

When Hitler came to power in Germany I decided to leave. I emigrated to Britain and arrived in London during November 1933. The extraordinary thing was that the complete break with my former way of life filled me with exhilaration rather than anxiety. I greatly enjoyed working for my living as a secretary in a film company. My grief, my distress and deep pain were knowing what was going on in Germany, what was happening to friends, to my father and my brother. It was also very bitter to experience the lack of concern here for what was occurring, and to be accused – when I said what was true – of being anti-Hitler simply because my father was a Jew.

I had ample time to think about things, about the dreadful outer events and the reaction of various countries and various individuals to the Fascist mass movement and to the violence that was unleashed and deliberately fostered. I began to look at myself, at my own violence and wish to retaliate, my hope of avenging myself on those who had killed – murdered – people I loved. I experienced great turmoil and did not know what to do. On Sundays, however, I used to go and sit for a while in some church. More and more I was drawn to the Brompton Oratory where I used to look at a lovely statue of Jesus pointing to His Sacred Heart. In my mind I spoke to this figure, and in my mind I heard Him speak to me. After quite some while I knew what I had to do and I became a Roman Catholic. Actually I did not 'become' a Catholic, for I realised that I had been one all my life. I had no difficulties with dogma; for me dogmatic statements were then, as they are now, expressions of inner truths experienced through the ages by different people in different ways and understood and verbalised from different levels. I was attacked by quite a number of people who could not understand why I wished to join a church at all, particularly one as rigid as the Roman. I was told of crimes committed through the centuries by the Church, the Popes, priests, monks and nuns. Such arguments seemed strange and irrelevant to me; I could not see the point of arguing such matters but only knew that I had stumbled upon my truth. What I did not know was that an archetype had been activated and a symbol had come to life in me. I was unconscious of their existence and unaware of such a formulation: for this I had to discover Jung.

I met Jung for the first time in 1927 at Darmstadt where I was attending an Easter School arranged by Hermann Keyserling on the theme of 'Man and Earth'. Jung spoke on 'Mind and Earth', but I understood very little of what he said. In fact when I sat next to him at dinner that evening I could not even ask any questions, for his ideas were far beyond my comprehension. Later it saddened me to think that I might have gone to Zürich then, and that Jung might have helped me to understand what had gone wrong in my marriage and what was wrong in my attitude to myself. It took ten more years, with all the upheavals in my outer and inner life, before I was ready to take in his ideas.

The first of Jung's books I read was *Modern Man in Search of a Soul*, suggested to me by a friend. It seemed to be the most important book that had ever come my way. The title itself rang a bell, and the various essays touched off thoughts which came up in a jumbled rush, all screaming for attention. At that time analysis was out of the question, partly for financial reasons, but also because I knew no-one connected with Analytical Psychology and was uncertain whether an analyst would consider taking me on. On the external level I was coping with my life. Then war broke out, and an Inspector from the CID came to interview me. One of his questions was why I had chosen to come to England, to which I replied that my father had had many friends here and my mother some relations. The official was satisfied, but I was not. I had given the right and acceptable answer to a difficult question, but I felt I had been accepted on the strength of my parents' connections and not for myself. My deliberate choosing of this country also seemed to have been invalidated, and as a consequence I felt invalidated myself.

This experience brought me one step nearer to having an analysis. My opportunity came in Oxford where I had joined friends during the very bad bombing of London. I met John Layard who was a Jungian analyst; he realised how much I needed analysis and suggested my analysing with him. I also joined groups interested in discussing Jungian theories and concepts. In due course, supervised by John Layard and Dr Kathleen Kitchin, founder of the Guild of Pastoral Psychology, I began to take patients myself. A little later Dr Rushforth, Medical Director of the Davidson Clinic in Edinburgh, asked me to join the Clinic as a member of the staff. At last, when the war was over, helped and encouraged by several friends, my dream of meeting Jung again came true.

My first interview with Jung was in Ascona at one of the Eranos meetings. He received me in a small flat which had been built for him above the lecture hall. This time I was in awe of Jung, for now I realised that he was the 'great wise old man' of psychology. I also looked at him much more carefully than I had before; he was tall, broad across the shoulders, and strongly built; the way he moved suggested that he was very much in control of his body. As he greeted me I was enchanted by the courtesy of his manner. We sat opposite each other and he looked at me with small, blue, penetrating eyes, holding his head in a way which showed how carefully he was listening.

Jung knew that I was working at a clinic in Edinburgh, but he did not know that I was also teaching psychology to prospective Catholic youth leaders under the Scottish Board of Education for the Ladies of the Grail. His interest was aroused, especially when I added that I was doing this from the angle of Analytical Psychology. He made me explain in detail how I had tackled this job; from the nature of his questions I realised that apart from his genuine interest, he wanted to discover how much I knew about and had understood his concepts. Jung saw me once more in Ascona, and then at regular intervals in Zürich when I had arranged for further training there. After three years in Zürich I returned to Edinburgh for a short time before settling in London permanently. Here I had some more analysis with Gerhard Adler and became a member of the Society of Analytical Psychology.

In Edinburgh I had worked alongside Freudian, Kleinian and Fairbairnian colleagues. I learnt a great deal from them, particularly the fact that their approach to the psyche was relevant and suitable, and corresponded to the workings of their own minds and to those of many others. My own mind did not work in this way, however, and I always found myself translating the much more concrete and medical terms into Jung's language. All his formulations have overtones and undertones which add a dimension by placing individual man within the whole context of the universe; heaven and earth, matter and spirit surround embodied, incarnate man who stands in the centre.

It was Jung's approach to the individual which meant so much to me. He did not think in terms of how somebody should be, but who he was. He attempted to understand the individual by studying the ways in which man had expressed his fears and his longings in the past. By including in his studies systems such as Alchemy, the I-Ching, Astrology and even Chirology which had been discredited by nineteenth- and twentieth-century men of science, Jung symbolically accepted man's dark, hidden spirituality and a kind of thinking which had been rejected. It was this attitude that gave me a sense of validity and of wholeness.

I have spoken about aspects of my life which represent not only my own experiences, but are common to all of us, though this may at first seem a strange idea as we struggle to work out relationships. We all have difficulties with our parents; we all have difficulties with partners; we are all afraid and lonely; we are all afraid of being angry, and yet 'anger is one of the sinews of the soul'; we are all looking for meaning in our lives, hoping to relate to that which is greater and stronger than we are or than any man is. Women have become restless, dissatisfied with the passive role allotted to them in the past, and seeking for a new identity. Above all, we all want to be loved and accepted and forgiven, and be helped to acknowledge and confess our weakness and shame. Over the years I have been asked to talk on some of these subjects from the psychological point of view and from the standpoint of Jung's teachings. For the purpose of this book I have looked at my talks, revising and re-writing or in some cases adding entirely new material. As a group these essays seem to me to be quite fundamental for bringing into consciousness facts that belong to the lives of all of us. To the lives of men as well as of women. We have to solve our problems in individual ways, but as our bodies are alike so are our psyches. We all walk, we may even all be able to dance, alone as well as in relationship, in rhythm with another, sometimes following, sometimes being followed.

> Tumult and peace, the darkness and the light –
> Were all like workings of one mind, the features
> Of the same face, blossoms upon one tree;
> Characters of the great Apocalypse,
> The types and symbols of Eternity,
> Of first, and last, and midst, and without end.
>   (Wordsworth : *Prelude*)

I owe a great debt of gratitude to Jung. Through him I learnt to look at myself without comparing what I was with something or someone else, without condemning myself, but as far as possible taking responsibility for my flaws. There are others whom I also thank for their help in enriching my understanding and my life: John Layard, Jolande Jacobi and Gerhard Adler who were my analysts. I shall always be intensely grateful to Winifred Rushforth, my chief in Edinburgh, whose generosity in giving me leave of absence enabled me to study in Zürich. Others, too numerous to mention, have also helped and encouraged me in ways I can never repay; I am deeply grateful, in fact, for having been so fortunate in the people I have met throughout my life.

# ASPECTS OF MAN

1 THE PARENT ARCHETYPE

The term 'archetype' was taken by Jung from St Augustine, and in his essay, 'The Mother Archetype', he defines it as synonymous with Plato's concept of the idea which pre-exists and is behind all phenomena. In the same essay Jung goes on to say that an archetype is the 'Urbild', the image, the capacity to form an image. An archetype is an empty form present in all human beings which is filled by each individual in a unique way, just as our instincts are capacities, possibilities which will be formed by the individual. An archetype can be recognised and named in principle. It will contain a kernel of meaning which does not vary, yet it will appear in all sorts of ways which do not depend on the archetype as such, but on personal factors. An archetype has innumerable aspects, personal and transpersonal, and can be benign or destructive, positive or negative.

The parent archetype is no exception. Like all other archetypes, the parent archetype appears in the creative fantasies, active imagination or dreams of the individual: and then it is projected, as a rule, on to the individual's parents. Collectively we find archetypes in myths and fairy tales: in our particular society we will find the parent in myths about father gods and mother goddesses, ultimately in the Great Father and the Great Mother. In fairy tales the parent archetype appears in the kings and queens, fairy godmothers and stepmothers, sorcerers and ogres.

It has been asserted that the divinities with which the heavens were peopled are projections. This is true, but it is very dangerous to add a 'nothing but' to this assertion, and to believe that thereby these powers have been dealt with and disposed of. No transpersonal power can be dealt with or disposed of by the intellect alone; projections have to be withdrawn, but this presupposes a conscious inner experience and the capacity to assimilate and accept as part of oneself contents which were conceived as being outside only. External 'debunking' can lead to being caught and overwhelmed by the image from within, from the unconscious.

Who then is the Great Mother who in Greece was called Hera and Hecate, Aphrodite and Demeter, and who has had many other names in the many countries of our world? She has always been connected with the moon and the earth, with darkness and the womb; she was and is the matrix from which all is born, from which all things come; the source of being, the deep unconscious from which consciousness emerges. In her benign aspect the Great Mother is therefore life, as it comes to be and burgeons; yet, being nature and ever desirous of fulfilling herself in the changing rhythm which is hers, she is sinister, too, and terrible. She is capable of devouring what she has brought forth, and re-absorbing into herself the life she gives – the womb no longer life-bearing, but life-destroying, prison and grave.

The father Gods are found in the heavens as the sun, as light and spirit; by their benign light we learn to choose, to discriminate and to become conscious of our actions and thoughts. But when they are fierce and roused in anger, they will annihilate us and burn us to ashes or dry up the marrow in our bones. Many myths describe how the world was created by the Great Mother, while others tell of the creation of the world by the Father; some again suggest that God and Goddess were united in silent embrace and everything was one, until suddenly they separated into above and below, into heaven and earth, into light and dark – into father and mother. Separation, this is the keyword for all creation.

The gods are creators in a cosmic sense, they are the father and mother of the world and all it contains, and it is their transpersonal power, which looms behind the human parent. The parent in turn creates the world and all it contains for the child, so that in a sense we face the gods when we regard our parents.

We know a good deal about the gods through the many stories that exist about them: they dwell in some heavenly place, for instance, and are to be feared; they are unpredictable, but they can be propitiated. They remain mysterious in their dealings, and seem to use their creatures for their own purposes. Moreover, they quarrel amongst themselves and are jealous of one another; often the gods lust after the daughters of men, and the goddesses are hungry for power.

All is one in the beginning of creation; all is one in the beginning for the child. Mother-father are one; everything is one. Then one day the great realisation of separation and distinction happens, the awareness of mother-father being two, not one. A new consciousness, a new and young ego is in the process of awakening. A new world comes into being, and it is the child who now creates his parents, by 'taking them in'. Perceiving them in external reality, he takes into himself an image which is already coloured by his experiences of external reality and by his parents' conscious attitude towards him. Of even greater significance for the child is the fact that he takes in all the longings and hopes, the fulfilments and frustrations, the love and hate that are alive in his parents' unconscious, and which have gone into the making of him – since he was conceived in body and in spirit.

This internalised image of the parent activates the archetype of the parent within the child. Experiencing his utter dependence, the child invests the parent with powers far surpassing human scope. This god-like aura, this mana, remains with the parent and constitutes the hold over the child which can hardly ever be completely broken. This is the transpersonal element in the child-parent relationship. On the personal level the child internalises his parents' hopes and expectations as demands. The introjected image therefore carries many 'oughts' with which the child identifies, so that he makes demands on himself from within long after they have ceased to be made from without. Nevertheless, for the individual those demands or ideas remain connected with the actual parents, and he may insist forever that they have to do only with the outside. Although outer influences may seem to have been overwhelming, they have an enduring effect only if there is a corresponding element within the child which responds and assents to a particular demand.

The parent does not only make demands, he also has qualities, possibly unpleasant ones. These, too, are mirrored in the child's inner image. For example, a parent may be cruel : as the child suffers from this cruelty he will reject the parent, eventually believing that he is thereby also rejecting the cruelty. This, however, need not necessarily be so, yet the individual may never realise that this distressing quality is not only without – in the parent – but also within himself. It is tragic that usually these truths are unrecognised, in other words the individual is unconscious of them. Insofar as he remains unconscious he will be unable to free himself from the parental image within and the actual parent without. He will be unable to differentiate between an inner image and external reality, between archetype and content. This means that a true relationship to the parent cannot be achieved, but remains an archetypal one : the parents are not humanised.

Here we are approaching the particular significance of the parent archetype. In the parent we encounter not only the first archetype, but also the first other human being. From the findings of psychological schools we know that this primal relationship is the basis for all relationship : for our relationship to God, to husband, wife and lover, and for the relationship to ourselves. Perhaps it is not sufficiently stressed that the primal relationship is also the basis for our relationship to our children. Actually the primal relationship to ourselves may be the acceptance of the unhappy and neglected child within. When this is forgotten, the parent cannot give his child the security of relationship as he does not know it himself. He is unconscious of the role he is playing and of his effect on and power over the child. The more uncertain and insecure the parent is in himself and in his role as parent, the more he will hide behind the cloak of omniscience and omnipotence and identify with the transpersonal archetype. The greater also will be the demands on the personal level, and the child's actual potentialities and character will be ignored and thwarted. Neither parent nor child confronts the other as he really is; they see each other through a distorting mirror. Whether the image they behold is fairer or fouler than reality, it is a fairy-tale one, illusory and unrelated to reality. It is a strange experience to realise how distorted an image a child can give of his parents, and how blind a parent can be about his child. How distorted, how blind, mean in effect how unconscious.

This is an important issue : the difficulty, the misfortune, the disaster in child-parent relationships result from being unconscious of what one is doing. Consciously the parent has to wear the archetypal cloak. Consciously he may have to oppose the child, providing him with an incentive to fight and enabling him to assent or dissent openly. Furthermore, the parent should allow the child to develop according to his own law, and should be understanding and loving – always. What about this last sentence? These are the archetypal demands and oughts made by the child on the parent. These and many more are made by children of all ages. Here the bondage of unconscious relationships comes full circle : the parent internalises these demands on him; the child is then a constant source of reproach and guilt. The parent takes to himself every difficulty, every frailty of the child as his own, nothing but his own responsibility. Again there is an unconscious identification with the super-human. Of course the parent carries responsibility, but no human being is solely the result of parental influence and environment.

We are apt to generalise and take sides, so I want to stress this: the child is a human being and the parent is a human being; there is no perfect child and no perfect parent. It seems, however, that precisely this idea – namely, of the perfect parent – is put before us in our religious teaching. The overstressing of the fourth commandment by religious teachers and by parents themselves has led to much unhappiness, and to fear and guilt, but not to the freedom and gladness of true relationship. The warning to parents uttered by St Paul, 'Do not rouse your children to resentment',[1] is rarely quoted, on the other hand, and I have never heard a sermon preached on this text. There is a strange saying by Jesus Himself in which he uses the concept of hate: 'If any man comes to me without hating his father and mother and wife and children and brethren and sisters, yes, and his own life too, he can be no disciple of mine'.[2] If, then, no-one can come to God who does not hate his parents, how can this be reconciled with the commandment, 'Honour thy father and mother'? I believe that the over-emphasising of what is due to the parent is based on the parent's insecurity. It seems to me that the commandment implies this: honour thy parents in spite of their frailty and their feebleness. It is through their human agency that 'I' am, therefore 'I' carry their frailties in myself – by 'honouring' them I honour myself, accept myself, and through this acceptance may be able to resolve some of the unresolved problems passed on to me. The command to honour, therefore, is a needful one: we have to honour our background and the substance of which we are made and which we carry within ourselves. But we also have to hate and fight the parent monster: the dragon that is always ready to devour us, the octopus which is forever squeezing us to death, the spider which is hungry for our blood.

In the New Testament we read that Jesus made His parents anxious. We also read that several times He said 'no' to His mother, a 'no' which had to be said; and – in an indirect way – we know how Mary reacted. It is a very difficult word to react to. When a child

[1] *Ephesians* 6, 2-4.   [2] *Luke* 14, 26.

is confronted with his first 'no' and the many 'nos' which follow, he is expected to learn to conform and obey, however difficult this may seem. It is possible that he will learn the lesson more quickly if his unconscious is not disturbed by his mother's resentment at some 'no' said to her. There is a tacit assumption that – psychologically speaking – parents are maturer than their child. This is not always so. Often a 'no' will rouse in the parent an emotional storm at being rejected and frustrated which equals the child's. So when the day comes on which the child intimates or speaks his first 'no' to his parent, the heartbreak and bewilderment may be great. Yet this 'no' has to happen and has to be expressed and experienced in various ways at the various stages of development.

'No' is the hero's word. It is the word of separation, of opposition to identification, it is an act of independence. It is an heroic act as its consequence could be loss of the affection which is prized more highly than anything else; it means that the primal parent-child relationship of identification is severed. It is an attempt to be born psychically, and this again is heroic since an attempt at independence and consciousness is always accompanied by feelings of guilt. It is an act which, when properly understood and dealt with, leads to the true human relationship between parent and child. Moreover, this act of separation surely is the 'hate' which has to be experienced before we can walk with God. There are many, however, who do not dare say 'no' to the parent, somehow hoping to remain forever in eternal security without responsibility. But their plight is greater and their feelings of guilt even more disturbing, for they have said 'no' to life. Nowadays we are all meant to be heroes and free ourselves from the bondage of the womb and the unconscious – a lot and privilege at one time reserved for the few. So one might wonder whether it was only lust which drove the father gods to the daughters of men. It was their offspring, the sons of these unions, who were the heroes and halfgods, fighting and overcoming the deadly danger of great dragons. The monsters who have to be fed the young, and those who attack and kill the young, are aspects of the terrible devouring Great Mother. They are symbols of the human parent who cannot let go. This parent has to be fought, yet all too often the monster has a terrible fascination for those who do not want freedom and who would rather 'blame' another than carry responsibility themselves. This is a crucial point, namely, to understand that such fascination stems from the Great Mother, from the transpersonal archetype operating both from within oneself and from the unconscious of the personal parent.

The title of this essay is 'The parent archetype', not 'The parents' archetype', and for a good reason. In the beginning the parents are one in the psyche. The small child telescopes his parents into one by investing the mother with the penis she took from the father. Mother-father are fused in the unconscious like the gods before the creation of the world. Like the gods, they have to separate, that is to say, they have to be differentiated in the psyche if creation is to follow. This means that the individual has to become conscious of the opposites, male and female, and also of father and mother within himself. It is only then that the union of father and mother within can take place. At this point we are confronted with a curious paradox: on the one hand the 'parent' is humanised and freed from the archetypal numinous aura, and the ego can stand secure in his own value; on the other hand the 'parent' within is transformed into the royal pair – king and queen of alchemy – and can be experienced as the Self in which all opposites are united. This *coniunctio oppositorum* is a religious experience in which through the Self we approach the Divine and are ourselves transformed, and transcending ordinary consciousness we may receive a glimmer of understanding of the meaning and purpose of things.

This ultimate union which is no longer fusion is the theme used in many representations of the supreme god where he is shown as a hermaphrodite. Such images are found among primitive people as well as among the most highly civilised. In Chinese and Japanese art the Goddess of Mercy, the Kwannon or Kwanyin, appears with a moustache, holding the Buddha child in front of her.

The same idea is at the back of our own religion. God the Creator, who created us male and female in His image, has been conceived therefore as being both male and female Himself. In many of the early representations of Our Lord He has a feminine-looking body. Dame Julian of Norwich called Jesus her Mother. Before the Incarnation the Son was the Logos, the wisdom of God. This aspect was also called Sophia. The following passage from Proverbs has been related to the Son, but also to Mary – so somehow the Son, Mary and Sophia are one. But also, the Son is the Father, and the Mother is the Bride :

The Lord possessed me in the beginning of his way, before his works of old.
I was set up from everlasting, from the beginning, ere ever the earth was.
When there were no depths, I was brought forth;
When there were no fountains abounding with water.
Before the mountains were settled, before the hills, was I brought forth....
When he prepared the heavens, I was there;
when he set a compass upon the face of the deep;
when he established the clouds above;
when he strengthened the fountains of the deep...
Then I was by him, as one brought up with him; and I was daily his delight,
playing always before him.

(Proverbs 8, 22–31)

The great fight against the parent archetype has to be fought with different weapons by the male and the female. The primal relationship of the male child to the mother is a heterosexual one, that is to say, it is a relationship of opposites. The mother is a woman and therefore alien to the son's nature, and so it is fatal for him to remain identified with her. His identification with the mother can only be broken by fighting and killing her; in mythology we find this idea expressed over and over again. The significance of this 'killing' is that the boy finds his manhood and is able to live his nature; but, curiously enough, it is also the means by which the mother herself transforms, and in the language of mythology, becomes benign. The primal relationship of mother-daughter is very different. There is no 'otherness' to contend with. Therefore it can be more difficult for the daughter to resolve her identification with the mother than it is for the son. The danger for her is that she will remain immature and infantile as long as she does not attempt to liberate herself, and this also means that she will be unable to have any relationships which are not based on identification. When she does start the fight it will be a long and arduous one: she may not 'kill' the Great Mother, she has to come to terms with her.

Dr Erich Neumann chose the perfect myth in the story of 'Amor and Psyche', by Apuleius, to show the feminine way of individuation. In the story, Psyche disobeys Amor, and her punishment consists in tasks put upon her by Amor's mother – the Great Mother – Aphrodite. The point is that Psyche has to obey the Great Mother; she is able to fulfil the tasks with the help of animals and plants. She is assisted by the eagle sent by the Great Father, Zeus, and even the stones of a tower speak to her, and she listens and understands them. She listens to her instincts, she is succoured by the spirit, and in the last and most dangerous task it is from the work of human hands – from humanity therefore – that she receives the helpful instructions. She fulfils all the tasks perfectly up to the end, and then at the last minute she fails! She opens the casket which is Aphrodite's and which she was to have handed over as she had received it. Dr Neumann sees this 'failure' as the climax of the story, because it is at that moment that Aphrodite forgives her. The relationship between the Great Mother and Psyche is achieved because Psyche has not only shown her indomitable spirit and courage, but also her femininity.

These fights against the parent archetype, unfortunately, have to be fought and have to be expressed in the personal sphere. These will be difficult times, they may be so difficult that both parents and children despair about one another. Both are fighting for survival. But it is a mistake to interpret the struggle as a purely personal one, for this can lead to the parent fearing the child as once the child feared him. This means that the archetype has not been faced, and then there will not be 'the tent and tabernacle of mutual forgiveness':

In Great Eternity every particular Form gives forth or Emanates
Its own peculiar Light; and the Form is the Divine Vision.
And the Light is his Garment. This is Jerusalem in every Man.
A Tent and Tabernacle of Mutual Forgiveness, male and female clothings.
And Jerusalem is called liberty among the children of Albion.

(*In Great Eternity,* Jerusalem. Blake)

I have said more about the archetypal mother than about the father. This has to do with the fact that we spring from the womb of the Great Mother and so it is she who is the archetypal parent. Her law is eternal and timeless, based on the rhythm of nature. Not so the law of the father which can change with time and in time. His is the world of the here and now; his is the will and the decision;

his is the world of the 'I'. And so his is also the sacrifice of the 'I'. God the Father is everliving in the death and resurrection of God the Son by the presence of God the Holy Ghost. We can also follow the lesson taught woman as mother in the new dispensation. The old mother goddesses were both benign and destructive; they were 'nature', following their instinctive urges. They were, so to speak, 'unconscious', and their desire was to keep mankind in the same condition. Mary was taught by her son: it may not have been easier for her than for many a human mother. Yet she learnt to look and be silent and to hold her physical motherhood to be naught. Then, in the end, she got her reward by being given the name and function of mother in the spirit – to be mother to him who had been loved by the son she bore, and through him to be mother of mankind.

2 ON THE ANIMUS

Jung discovered in the course of his work with patients that the psyche contains contra-sexual elements. Freud was also aware of this phenomenon, but he did not study it in any depth.

Jung found that men and women project images onto one another which correspond to their own contra-sexual make up, and that these images appear in dreams personified in definite figures: they stem from the deep unconscious, they belong to the structure of the psyche, and therefore are archetypal. Archetypes are experienced in images and when constellated they affect consciousness. Jung called the feminine archetype in man anima, and the masculine in woman animus. The Latin word *anima* means soul; but Jung did not mean the soul in the Christian dogmatic sense. Anima, according to Latin philosophic ideas, refers to the dark feminine side of being. It is in this sense that the anima is man's soul.

For some time there was confusion about the term 'animus'; Jung used it about woman as if it were her masculine soul, and speaks about soul-images when either the anima or the animus are projected onto actual people or onto figures in dreams. Mrs Jung was instrumental in correcting this mistake; she pointed out that the animus is spirit, and the characteristic of spirit is movement and activity.

Once, from nursery days onwards, men and women had no doubts about their inherent physiological and psychological differences; a little girl played with dolls and felt herself to be their mother; a little boy played with soldiers and felt himself to be their commander. A woman was expected to be pretty and a little silly, whereas a man was supposed to be forceful and reliable.

These ideas are no longer valid in the outer world, but in the inner world the image of man being strong and woman weak still operates as an expectation which man projects on to woman, and woman on to man. The bitterness of woman's disillusionment when she discovers the man's weakness, and man's resentment when he encounters her strength have led to uncertainty in relationships and confusion about the nature of the difference between the sexes. In individual cases women may seem to enjoy their power, but underneath we often find unhappiness. This is particularly true today, perhaps, with the upsurge of 'women's lib' and the resultant confusion of roles.

Man and woman, masculine and feminine are complementary opposites : on the biological level, the quick, volatile sperm fertilises the passive slow-moving ovum which nourishes the fruit and envelopes it till it can be born. To complement means to complete or rightly coexist with something : the anima and the animus are the complements which by rightly coexisting complete a personality.

The anima's function is to soften man's one-sided analytical attitude and the over-bright critical light he sheds on his environment with which he can so easily annihilate woman. The anima is man's muse who inspires him throughout life, she leads him – expressed in the terms of one of the greatest poets – through Hell and Purgatory to Heaven. But, when woman and the feminine have been experienced too negatively and in consequence the anima is so feared that she is repressed, ignored or despised, she makes her presence felt by turning a man into a moody, irritable, maladjusted, vain and effeminate person.

Unfortunately these few words about the anima have to suffice, because the main concern here is with the animus.

The archetype of the animus is first and foremost masculinity as such. His function is to bring light into the woman's lunar and diffuse attitude to life; he kindles her capacity to differentiate and separate, and leads her to greater consciousness; he quickens her into activity; he initiates her into deeper levels of understanding and to a sense of the meaning of life. This positive, creative aspect of the animus only operates when an established ego exists which can confront him. It is true that archetypes are autonomous complexes and act independently of ego, will or intentions, but nevertheless the ego can have a willingness to confront these tremendous, numinous powers from the unconscious. In the case of the animus there is a very particular difficulty : many women are more unaware of his presence than a man may be of the anima, and in that case a woman cannot confront him; she may know of his existence theoretically and yet not realise when he is playing her up.

The animus is not only a personification of masculine qualities, he also carries the ideas, the hopes, the wishes, the fears women have had about man all through the ages : man, the hero in all his strength and glory to whom one wants to belong body and soul; man, the seducer into whose arms one falls; man, the monster from whom one shrinks in trembling disgust; man, the teacher who opens the heavens; man, the father who is the great and tender protector. These attributes all belong to the collective animus, but such expectations are modified by personal experiences with the father from earliest childhood, (who is usually the first man to carry archetypal projections) and then with brothers or any other men in an individual woman's environment. The father is particularly important : in infancy he is experienced only as background to mother through her relationship to him. His attitude to life in general, his thoughts, his morals and ideals filter through at a preconscious level and are part of an unconscious conditioning of the animus. There may or may not have been a dramatic clash between father and daughter, yet there is always some disillusionment with regard to the first man one falls in love with. It is from this deep level of early disappointment, augmented by collective archetypal fear, that much unconscious hostility against man springs. It depends on an individual's reaction to pain, on its nature and its depth, what happens to the animus, as he is not only a type, a collective, immutable entity, but a dynamic living process in the psyche of an individual.

A dynamic living animus presupposes an ego which can confront him, who is consciously aware of him, which means that ego and animus are separated from one another and have space between them. All too often, however, instead of having an animus, a woman is possessed by him. The process of being swallowed by the animus begins in childhood, when a girl feels she has to defend herself against her parents, or her environment, or both. Her aggression may go outwards against others, or it may go inwards against herself; in either case it is the animus who stands in front of the ego. The animus is experienced as a shield, but unfortunately the ego cannot develop behind it : animus and ego get mixed up and the result is a very vulnerable paranoiac ego. Endeavours to make this situation conscious are desperately resisted, because there is the fear that a separation of ego and animus will lead inevitably to a total collapse of the personality. This state of possession by the personal animus shows itself when a woman becomes his mouthpiece: she is stuck in opinions, vehemently reflecting or opposing her father's attitudes, or even worse, her mother's animus idea. Shoulds and oughts abound in her vocabulary; she is moralistic, if not for others, certainly for herself; she is perfectionist and ambitious, overcritical, again particularly of herself though also of others. It is therefore difficult for her to make relationships, and to keep them up when 'disillusioned'. Such a woman may be given to good works in an interfering way, so that people come to fear and dislike her. Outwardly bossy, inwardly insecure and uncertain of herself a woman then hides behind pronounced aggressiveness, and so the animus is badly contaminated with shadow qualities; the woman, unconscious of what it is that is possessing her is often quite unable to understand why she is shunned and why her capabilities are not appreciated.

Apart from the personal animus who can possess a woman there is also the animus in his collective aspect who holds women in general in his grip. In our patriarchal society women had to fight for their freedom; when they discovered capacities in themselves which had been attributed previously only to men they were understandably proud; they were also anxious to prove themselves always and in every situation equal to men, and so they identified with the envied masculine qualities – the collective animus – and to a large extent lost awareness of the value and validity of their femininity.

Identification with any one part of oneself is dangerous; identification with the contra-sexual archetype leads to the condition Freud called narcissism: in Jungian language this signifies that the image, anima or animus, is not projected onto another, a person cannot 'fall in love', because he is too identified with, too much in love with, his own other side.

The late Dr Michael Rosenthall had an interesting theory. He thought that projections made by an infant on the loved and hated primary objects, the breast and the penis in Kleinian language, correspond to an archetypal image of a much more primitive kind than the soul image; but he believed that this early projection can lead to a mature image of the contra-sexual archetype if the process is not prevented by envy being too strong. In other words, if because of envy the contra-sexual archetype is not constellated, the personality remains infantile and unfulfilled: only through the process of projection, through transference and counter-transference can infantile patterns be corrected; in the dynamics of give and take, withdrawal and giving out, an individual can grow to be a personality.

Another aspect of the animus is connected with a woman's latent male sexual characteristics. Jung comments on this in *Symbols of Transformation*, though he does not use the term animus; speaking about Miss Miller's fantasy figure, the young hero Chiwantopel, he says: 'The figure of Chiwantopel is the portion of the libido bound up with the mother (and therefore masculine); hence he is her infantile personality, the childishness of character which, as yet, is unable to understand that one must leave parents in order to save the total personality.' It is the animus who is tied up with the mother, the animus who promotes incestuous desires from daughter to mother and from mother to daughter, and it is the animus who stands behind female homosexuality.

Lastly: the animus is spirit, is logos, is the word: it is he who initiates woman into the otherness of male spirit: on the personal plane through the experience of love for a man; on the transpersonal plane by making her receptive to the numinous.

From these remarks it is clear that the figure of the animus is very powerful and ambivalent: he is personal and transpersonal; he is positive and negative; as an archetype he is amoral, collective, impersonal. As the personal animus he can enlighten, and he can obscure: he may talk about opinions instead of communicating thoughts; he can strengthen the ego and bring about independence, but he also can over-emphasise a woman's sense of power and desire to dominate; he can lead the soul to a deeper level of insight, and he can hinder any progress by holding on to preconceived ideas. The animus can be experienced as a presence, as a voice or as spirit: primitive woman conceived from him in the flesh; modern woman can conceive from him the psyche; but if a woman falls for his demonic fascination he can lead her away into the clouds and take her from an appreciation of reality into a cloud-cuckoo land of inflation and neurosis.

Women's ambivalence with regard to the animus can be seen in dreams: he appears as the husband, lover, or brother; or as a total stranger or as a man one had not thought of for a long time; sometimes two such men play a part in the same dream: one helpful, the other destructive. A known or unknown man may be frightening, disgusting, raping, treacherous in a dream one night, and in the next night a figure appears who conveys a sense of utter peace and completion. Dreams in which a woman is very frightened by a raping man may show that she is split in her attitude to man and therefore is incapable of being wholly satisfied in sexual intercourse: she cannot give herself for fear of being annihilated, she cannot let man in for fear of being hurt too much. It is significant that it is not always easy to distinguish between the helpful and the destructive animus; the ego of the dreamer in dream and in consciousness is not always very reliable! In the long run, however, as understanding of the conflict which underlies every external problem deepens, it becomes easier to differentiate between these exponents of the unconscious, and to realise which one – if it is only one – is the true leader of the soul, the true psychopompos.

There is a well-known group of dreams in which a woman has to face a plurality of men : a court of justice, a court martial, a court consisting of very old men or priests. The woman knows that she is to be judged for a crime she has committed, yet she herself does not know what it is she has done. The collective sentence which is pronounced on her, though the woman may wake from the dream before this happens, is felt to be in the nature of condemnation. This shows how much a woman is subject to collective, conditioned moralistic judgments connected with the past and the father world; if such dreams are made use of so that through greater consciousness a woman is able to understand, and becomes capable of observing her reactions in situations which arouse her feelings of guilt, she may be able to free herself eventually from the angry, threatening collective animus.

A moralistic attitude may be emphasised by a masochistic streak so that a woman cannot stop attacking herself with feelings of guilt; condemnatory dreams may be related, therefore, to dreams in which the dreamer finds herself in physical danger, being persecuted by a gang of hooligans or coshers; the dreamer is usually thoroughly frightened in such dreams, and so she will either make an attempt to run away or she will try to defend herself : then she may find a helper in the figure of one man; from this occurrence an awareness can dawn that the great danger to the ego lies in the collective nature of some attitude.

The plurality of animus figures in a dream is not paralleled for the anima : a man is never condemned or exalted by a court of women.

In spite of the social change in the status of women, the dreams of 'many men' still persist. I am inclined to think that this has to do with woman's capacity to think in images, and the fact that in a patriarchal society most judges, all priests, all the elders and most soldiers are in fact men. Jung has something else to say which is very interesting:

'With regard to the plurality of the animus as distinguished from what we might call the "uni-personality" of the anima, this remarkable fact seems to me to be a correlate of the conscious attitude. The conscious attitude of woman is in general far more exclusively personal than that of man. Her world is, in general, made up of fathers and mothers, brothers and sisters, husband and children. The rest of the world consists likewise of families, who nod to each other but are, in the main, interested essentially in themselves. The man's world is the nation, the state, business concerns, etc. His family is simply a means to an end, one of the foundations of the state, and his wife is not necessarily the woman for him (at any rate not as the woman means when she says "my man"). The general means more to him than the personal; his world consists of a multitude of co-ordinated factors, whereas her world, outside her husband, terminates in a kind of cosmic mist. A passionate exclusiveness therefore attaches to the man's anima, and an indefinite variety to the woman's animus. Whereas the man has, floating before him, in clear outlines, the significant form of a Circe or Calypso, the animus is better expressed as a bevy of Flying Dutchmen or unknown wanderers from over the sea, never quite clearly grasped, protean, given to persistent and violent motion. These expressions appear especially in dreams, though in concrete reality they can be famous tenors, boxing champions, or great men in faraway, unknown cities.'[1]

This is no longer true: the woman's world no longer terminates in a sort of cosmic mist; and there are no more bevies of Flying Dutchmen; boxers and great men in faraway countries are replaced by the Beatles and the like who send the young into screaming ecstasies. On the whole, much younger men attract the young girl than was formerly the case: this may be due partly to economic factors. Older men are frankly referred to as 'sugar daddies' and used in this capacity. The myth of monogamous woman has also been exploded: it is not only 'her man' on whom she focusses;

[1] C. W. Volume 7, page 208, *The Relations between the Ego and the Unconscious.*

her children, particularly her sons, were always the husband's rivals; now she often has a profession which holds her interest. Even in the sexual field she can and does go further than she used to as the tradition upheld by woman's persona has made way for new conventions.

It is interesting to note, however, that the animus figure in dreams of girls and young women who live a less restricted sexual life than their more restrained or even sexually repressed sisters, tends to be much less colourful. Young married women frequently meet an animus in their dreams who is drear, weak, half impotent, possibly even effeminate; angry, disappointed comments on this figure include statements like: 'he is exactly like my husband'. Wives often complain bitterly about their husband's 'weakness'; they feel that he does not defend them, or that he does not shut them up when they know that they are nagging, and worst of all, a husband does not have a row with them when they have fairly far-going flirtations with other men.

There have always been animus-ridden women who longed to be freed from his yoke, but the trouble now is even more acute. Whatever women have fought for, in their personal relationships they want to feel protected by a man who is at least as strong as they are possibly stronger and able to hold them. Yet, generally speaking, women choose their husbands and lovers, and if he is ineffectual it is a reflection on the woman's animus as there is a correspondence between inner reality and projection. Uncertainty and impotence exist in the woman just as much as they do in the man, and unless this is recognised the man and the woman make each other frigid and impotent. It is interesting to turn to literature and compare animus figures in novels written by women of earlier periods with those of today.

In the late eighteenth century the hero was dark-haired, gaunt, with deep-set eyes, ascetic and yet irresistibly attracted to women and they to him: the prototype of the Romantic ideal of man. In the nineteenth century we have Rochester, Charlotte Brontë's hero, his dark demonic ugliness, and his sadism; Heathcliff, Emily Brontë's soul image, was the mysterious stranger brought into the house by the father, untamed, evil and cruel. At the same time both the sisters offset their heroes with another figure: in Charlotte's case with a fanatically religious one, in Emily's with a weak and amiable one. Modern heroes belong to a totally different order; apart from the anti-hero who evokes a woman's protective instincts, we find the detective hero who is aristocratic, chivalrous, good-looking, who always discovers the real criminal and sees to it that justice is done. Only one of these detectives is a comic-looking foreigner who solves crimes with the help 'of the little grey cells', with the help of the thinking function, in other words. All these men have one thing in common : almost always they have to work against the official police; it is one man, one animus, against collective faulty justice.

From the stories written for the two most popular women's magazines, it transpires that women consider doctors to be the ideal marriage partners, architects and advertising executives follow in popularity. In these stories there are no divorcees; actual sex is never mentioned; hardly any woman is really interested in a career; material worries do not exist, only emotional ones; most girls are secretaries and give up their jobs on marriage. These stories correspond to fairy stories, for women know very well that life is different; this becomes obvious from the letters they write to these magazines asking for advice and from the type of answers they get.

Man's soul image, his anima, has not changed to the same extent : he always wanted the child wife and he still does. Baby Doll, the kittenish woman, arouses his sexuality; speaking in a very general way, man feels that he can cope with a child – even though he often cannot emotionally. He fears woman as a rival; all too often she has not given him a sense of his masculinity, but on the contrary – so he feels – she has emasculated him.

Rivalry between woman and man contains much fear, jealousy and envy. Woman's penis envy has made way for man's breast envy; women no longer need envy men, nor is the feminine protest necessary. Women take pride in their achievements in the professional field, particularly those which used to be masculine prerogatives; these are put in front of the shop window, whereas feminine achievements, even childbearing and certainly all domestic pursuits, are put in the backroom : the result is a disturbing psychic change of sex, disturbing for both man and woman.

In spite of the fact that to a great extent woman has achieved an equal status with man, there is still an over-emphasis on being masculine; a sense of value and meaning which belongs to femininity has got lost. Yet there is a curious difference between the older and the younger generation; the older never doubted the existence of opposite attitudes in men and women, though they had, and have, to learn to recognise the validity of the feminine point of view. The problem of the young generation seems to consist in discovering that opposites exist which have to be separated and differentiated. The woman's disappointment with man as sexual partner and as true and equal companion, plus the realisation that professional work does not bring total satisfaction, are at the back of many of her feelings of emptiness, bitterness and meaninglessness. The two lives which so many women lead nowadays, their need to be efficient in the professional field and their equal need to lead a satisfactory emotional and home life, have produced a split which is not easy to bridge. Women can only find this bridge in that aspect of the animus whose function it is to be a bridge, and who can show her the way to the meaning of life.

It is not only today that illusions in relationship with a loved person get lost; it has always happened, and it has always been heroic to look at one's love, for fear that this love who is one's god will disappear. The fear may be so great that it leads to the fallacy of believing that it is easier and better to hold on to a fantasy image: it is not better, because the day comes when a fantasy is bound to be destroyed, and then real damage is the result. Therefore a risk is more fruitful though it can be painful and difficult. In the myth of Amor and Psyche, Psyche took the risk. She faced love, and seemingly lost it for ever. She was, however, willing to work and fight for it. Several tests had to be performed in which helpful animals and plants gave her advice: her instincts helped her through. But then the tower, man-made and impersonal. gave her advice on how to behave in the underworld. Psyche obeyed the tower up to a point, then, at the last moment she forgot the male principles and impulsively followed her female curiosity: at that moment she was reconciled to the mother goddess, and regained her love.

Essentially the animus problem is bound to remain the same at all times though it may appear in different forms. To achieve a personal, individual position, collective attitudes have to be sacrificed. This is no mean task as it also involves the dissolving of projections. Such a sacrifice may be experienced in a dream as a demand made by an animus figure, or simply as an image; then the dream can be a nightmare. In the waking appraisal the reaction may be almost hysterical in the degree of terror shown and the utter rejection of the demand. However, when a dream with such a demand has been remembered and dreamt to the end, it may be possible for the ego eventually to let go of the fear of being destroyed by such a sacrifice : the significance of the ordeal can be understood and the demand fulfilled.

The animus likes living in the twilight; he is really a psychological function, but he retains a personality as long as his contents are unconscious and he is not used purposefully. Woman is still afraid of man : on one level she will always be because of the archetypal fear of being invaded, assaulted, raped and destroyed by him. She is afraid of him, therefore, whatever her personal experiences may have been : her great fear now is that man's power and fascination will keep her 'imprisoned in the darkness of instinctual life'. Her danger is to fall from the outer fascination of prison, into the inner one : purposeful use of the animus can only come about through a conscious confrontation of ego here – animus there.

Jung says : 'The femininity pertaining to the man and the masculinity pertaining to the woman, the experience man has of woman and vice versa can be integrated into the personality by the process of conscious realisation. The masculine and feminine archetypes, however, cannot.'

This means that masculine and feminine remain opposites – and therefore there will remain tension between woman and man : this tension is the basis of life from which life can spring; here is the mystery of the desire for union : the *mysterium coniunctionis*.

3 PSYCHIC ENERGY

The concept of Psychic Energy is one of the most important in Analytical Psychology, as it is connected with the whole of life and all its conflicts. The subject has so many facets, however, that only a few can be touched upon here.

For those who work in the field of psychology the concept has the particular significance of having been the main controversial issue on which the friendship between Freud and Jung foundered. Jung used the term 'psychic energy' for the first time in 1907 in the introduction to his paper *The Psychology of Dementia Praecox*, the illness which is now called schizophrenia. He wished to convey the idea of a general interest in and desire for life, and then describe a stage in schizophrenia in which a patient retreats completely from external reality. Jung had to avoid the term 'libido' at that time, because Freud had employed it in his *Three Essays on the Theory of Sexuality*, published in 1905, solely in the sense of sexual drive.

Freud was so struck by Jung's paper that he invited him to Vienna. Friendship and collaboration ensued and lasted for about five years. From the start, however, Jung voiced his reservations about, and raised objections to, the exclusiveness of Freud's sexual theories. For Freud, libido, life instinct and sexuality were synonyms; according to him, libido, which is the basis of all feeling and emotion, springs from primitive eroticism, and even when its primary aim is lost and another substituted, it remains sexuality. Freud insisted on this tenet, which meant that he was extending the word 'sexuality' far beyond the common usage. He attributed Jung's doubts to lack of experience; this was true, Jung remarked later, for he was younger: he was the son, and Freud was the father. But greater experience created ever greater doubts in Jung's mind, arising in particular from his research into schizophrenia.

He became more and more convinced that in schizophrenic withdrawal from external reality, instincts are involved which cannot be called sexual, and, in his words, 'external reality is more than a function of sexuality'. Finally, Jung decided that the time had come to put his own views forward. He did so in his first major book, *The Psychology of the Unconscious*, which is a study of the dreams and fantasies of an American schizophrenic woman. The book was published in 1912; in 1950 Jung revised it under the title of *Symbols of Transformation*.

In this book, Jung expounded his theories on the nature of the unconscious, and his ideas on the transpersonal aspect of the parents, emphasising the importance of the mother in her positive as well as in her devouring, castrating aspect. Furthermore, he re-appraised the terms 'psychic energy' and 'libido'. By using the term 'psychic energy', Jung had been stressing the energic aspect of the great unknown force which pervades all human activity, and this enabled him to explain functional disturbances other than sexual ones more satisfactorily. But he re-interpreted the term 'libido' according to the original classical definition of the word which was in line with his use of the term 'psychic energy'; from then on he used 'libido' and 'psychic energy' synonymously. Freud was outraged, particularly by Jung's incorporating the term 'libido' into his system; he took Jung's book as a betrayal of himself and of his teaching. He expelled Jung from the Psycho-Analytical Society and he never forgave him.

Jung had foreseen this possibility. He had called the last chapter of his book 'The Sacrifice'. The sacrifice consists in the cutting of the incestuous tie binding one to the parent, and the letting go of the infantile longing for the security of the womb. It is facing the fear of being alone. It is the willingness to carry feelings of guilt by not meeting the demands and the expectations made by external parents, parent-figures, or by their inner equivalents. Whilst he was writing this chapter, Jung was conscious that he himself was bringing the sacrifice; by 'betraying' Freud he took upon himself the stigma of disloyalty to a revered father-figure.

The rift between Freud and Jung was tragic as every rift is which occurs between father and son, between parents and children, or between friends. Yet it sometimes seems as if only through such emotional unheavals can sufficient energy be released for an individual to be able to assert himself.

Libido or psychic energy is the urge towards life, and is comparable with the concept of energy in physics. Jung thought that the reproductive instinct, together with the protective one, were the most prominent instincts at the dawn of human life. Once man had established himself, energy which had gone into the propagation and the preservation of life found new outlets. Consciousness emerged, and the instinct of self-preservation developed with the appearance of the ego. Self-preservation aims at defending the individual's interest and bestows a sense of personal importance and power whereas the sexual and the protective instincts are not always consistent with the individual's welfare.

Sex and power are opposites; on a primitive, unconscious level they manifest themselves as complementary drives such as, for instance, the bodily needs of feeding and excreting; on more conscious levels, however, these two insincts of giving and taking are often at war. This experience of conflict is essentially the tension between ego and shadow.

Jung deliberately refrained from calling any instinct the 'greatest'. He spoke of libido as an energetic value that could show itself as power, hunger, sexuality or religion. Every instinct exists in its own right and cannot be reduced to another one. Each one can remain in an infantile state and overwhelm an individual by the sheer strength of its drive; but it can also be repressed or suppressed by an individual or collectively by society.

The most repressed instinct at the moment is the drive behind the search for the meaning and significance of life in general, and one's own life in particular. Repressed psychic energy does not cease to exist; on the contrary, it becomes a disruptive factor breaking through into personal or collective consciousness in strange ways and disturbing symptoms. With the co-operation of the ego lost energic value can be brought back into consciousness and become available to the ego-personality.

Every instinct is a particular kind of energy, but it is the tension between them that makes for life. The greater the tension the greater the capacity for any form of activity. In practice, tension should not be greater than the ego can tolerate; the result of excessive tension is to create great everyday difficulties, and a feeling of being torn and paralysed. This excessive tension can be diminished, but sometimes those who suffer from it believe that all tension should disappear, or sometimes they are secretly proud of and attached to their swing of moods. When, however, a new attitude to life and to the various values in oneself gradually unfolds, there may be all the more stability the more violent the conflict was. Stability is not standstill. Stability means that energy is freed for tasks other than waging inner war : excessive warfare is unnecessary once the validity of opposing drives has been recognised. Standstill in contrast means cessation of movement : no energy is generated, and this is death – psychological if not physical.

In the inner world instincts are often represented by animals. There are many myths, legends and fairy stories which tell of helpful animals. They also appear in dreams and are benevolent, threatening or persecuting according to the dreamer's disposition towards the particular creature.

All through the ages from antiquity to the present age, the horse has personified power and energy. In several civilisations it was associated with the supreme god or mother-goddess, and was sacrificed to them. It was said to have powers of divination and was held in awe. In Greek mythology there are happier overtones : Apollo's horses speed around the sun. Poseidon's steeds gallop over the sea, and the winged horse is the poet's inspiration. Energy in the minds of men is shown to have two aspects : on the one hand the horse as forward – striving towards continual renewal, and on the other, there is the mare, generating fear which may turn to panic and death.

The intimate relationship which exists between man and horse becomes apparent in the Greek myth of the centaurs, beings who are half-man and half-horse; the most famous among them – Cheiron – was wise, a prophet and a healer. The idea of man and horse being a unity also occurs as a concept in Eastern philosophy and in occult thought; interestingly enough, it has suddenly appeared most forcefully in modern sculpture.

The Italian sculptor Marino Marini has been almost obsessed by the theme horse and rider; over and over he shows them belonging together in joy and in despair. His greatest work is the one he called 'Il Miracolo', the Miracle. The work depicts a huge horse reared up, sitting on his haunches, his head turned to the right in agonised wonder; the rider is falling backwards, holding on to the horse with his legs, his head lifted up and his arms outstretched in an attitude of prayer. Marini intended to show the miracle of man and beast, both seeing and recognising the majesty of an otherworldly power; he actually had in mind the conversion of St Paul.

The horse carries man, can run away with him and throw him; it is the irrational instinctive side of man which can be very close to the spirit. The rider is the rational side, capable of directing and guiding instinctive forces, but also the part which can be either too sure or too unsure of itself. When the intellect over-directs, the horse gets stubborn and difficult; as soon as the attitude of intellectual superiority is relinquished, instinctive wisdom can take over and co-operate with reason. When man under-directs he remains dominated by instinctive fears and desires. Identification with either side, whether the intellectual or the instinctive one, leads to complications and often to psycho-somatic symptoms.

All through his life Jung was exercised by, and wrestled with, the problem of energy, as can be seen in his writings. He recognised that the psyche is subject to the same kind of laws as matter is, namely to the causal and to the energetic. They are like two ends of a stick. The causal law is mechanistic: every event is due to a cause, therefore past events govern the present and the future is determined by such events. This is the 'because' in life; 'because' environment, parents, etc., were as they were, I am bound to be this or that: it is the past which conditions. The energic law is final, which means flowing towards a goal, though the goal is unknown. The psyche is in continuous motion, constantly attempting to keep psychic contents in balance. It is energy that underlies movement, and all change; energy makes change possible; it is the 'perhaps', the unknown, the unexpected that happens in life.

Whilst Jung was stressing the energic point of view more and more, atom and quantum physicists made discoveries which shattered all the old notions of the nature of matter and of the universe. Purely causal explanations, strict determinism and fixed laws were no longer tenable once the principles of indeterminacy and probability had to be accepted. Matter is not solid and indestructible, but a concentrated form of energy. Time and space are relative. Energy is the main principle operating in the universe; its source is unknown, but it is known by its effects. Because of these discoveries, thinking in terms of a four-dimensional universe became a necessity.

Jung drew conclusions from this new way of thinking, although he was unable to produce a mathematical formula for the psyche as the physicists had done for matter. He showed how the relativity of time and space is the basis from which para-psychic phenomena become understandable, so that a stratum of experience, which until recently was considered to be due to mental instability, has become scientifically respectable. A psyche touches matter at some point, and matter has a latent psyche; this was a belief widely held in antiquity and in the middle ages. Jung argues that there is either a pre-established harmony of physical and psychic events, or physical and psychic events are in a state of interaction. The viewpoint of pre-established harmony is the deterministic one. The hypothesis of interaction is the energic point of view and is an idea that goes beyond space and time in a three-dimensional world; it is a new concept which is connected with the four-dimensional universe as postulated by physicists. This new principle which Jung stipulated is the principle of meaningful coincidences, or synchronicity as he also called it. Interaction of psyche and soma became axiomatic to Jung; he began to look at illness in this light, and became suspicious of psychosomatic explanations which only take casual factors into account.

He knew from his own experience that illness need not only be an expression of a faulty psychic adaptation, but that it can be a time of incubation from which new insight is born; meaningful coincidences happen within the psycho-somatic unity of the human being. Jung went very far in his speculations about man, he even hinted at the possibility that synchronicity was the principle by which man's two natures come together at birth.

It is bewildering to follow these ideas and difficult to think of the principle of psychic energy as a parallel to energy in physics. Atom physicists have been able to concretise their findings; the proof for the validity of their theories is the bomb. Jung uncovered the dangerous bomb in the psyche, but man is still very unconscious of its being within himself, and goes on blaming 'others' for any explosion that happens. Ego experience has separated us from others, from our fellow-men, from creatures, things and events. Jung showed that through that part of our being which underlies the ego we are intimately connected with the existing universe. External reality and conscious attitude, inner reality and our attitude to this and to ourselves, our way of life, all together make for the wholeness of our being. Jung added a further dimension to our knowledge of ourselves and breached the dangerous split between the material world and the world of the psyche; much more consciously than ever before man can feel himself to be one with, to be responsible to and for the universe we live in.

4 PERSONAL ENTHUSIASM

When I was recently asked to speak on personal enthusiasm I agreed to do so, but I soon discovered a conflict within myself. Every time I attempted to think about what I was going to say, my mind seemed to go blank, and I felt uneasy. I became aware of strong misgivings about the subject; at the same time I know myself what it feels like to be enthusiastic – to be 'high'. One realises the tremendous appeal of feeling one has an aim, and life may become meaningful. And also one realises how tragic it would be if all romanticism and all high spirits were to disappear.

Yet to me, enthusiasm is very problematical. I know that a feeling called gratitude exists and a joyful attitude to life, though these have become very rare. In *Look Back in Anger*, John Osborne has Jimmy Porter say: 'How I long for a little ordinary human enthusiasm. Just enthusiasm – that's all. I want to hear a warm, thrilling voice cry out Hallelujah! Hallelujah! I'm alive!'

There are some privileged people of genius who are able to evoke such feelings: teachers who kindle a spark in those who are in their care – young or old – when they teach how to see and how to hear, when they open minds to the excitement of learning, and hearts to the enchantment of beauty. This kind of enthusiasm – being carried away by the word, by sound, by love, by the sun and the moon and the stars – surely is to be inspired by a god, God? But in spite of all his enthusiasm the teacher must have knowledge, skill and consciousness.

My unease persisted: the inflationary aspect of enthusiasm, the one-sidedness, the fanaticism, the obstinacy connected with it were constantly at the back of my mind, and also the awareness that enthusiasm and ecstasy need not have only the beautiful, good or true as their object or aim. For some time now we have seen enthusiasm and ecstasy aroused in people when they are confronted with the ugly or the obscene – with the shadow side.

A film I saw emphasised my negative feelings and became a focus for them; a discussion with friends clarified my ideas further, as in speaking I had to clarify at least some of my thoughts.

The film is called *Cabaret* and is based on some Isherwood stories about Berlin in the early nineteen-thirties. It shows a vicious, corrupt, permissive society whose main values were money and sex on the one hand, and on the other the beginnings of the Nazi movement with all its violence, sadism and cruelty whose values consisted in the idea of the supremacy of the Nordic race – the blond beast – and in the wielding of power. The film also shows that which is between these two worlds and that which connects them: despair, fear, death – I'm not sure. But it is very frightening to see. In one of the most chilling scenes I have ever seen on the screen, a beautiful, blue-eyed, fair-haired boy stands and sings 'Tomorrow belongs to me'; he is in Nazi uniform, and in that beer garden on a lovely summer's evening, slowly, one by one, people get up to join in the singing, fervently and enthusiastically. The debauched society may have been satanic, and yet artistically and intellectually it was outstanding; the new movement which aroused enthusiasm and was out to awaken the people from their sleep and apathy was luciferian in its power to seduce by terror and blackmail.

I told friends about the film; some understood my reaction, but one woman in particular was surprised. She said that the people's response to the song had not been a manifestation of enthusiasm, but a kind of mass-hysteria activated by the beautiful youth who, though sincere, was himself a victim of his idealism. This, however, is precisely what enthusiasm is all about. The original Greek meaning of the word was: to be possessed, or to be inspired by a god – slightly different from 'invaded'. The German word *Begeisterung*, echoes this: bespirited. In English 'enthusiasm' was once a term used for fanatically religious people, and 'enthusiast' was a word of abuse for those outside the mainstream of the Church.

The religious connotations of the concept of enthusiasm have got lost in modern usage; now when we speak of enthusiasm we mean whole-hearted devotion to an ideal or to a cause, or single-mindedness in a pursuit or a study, or hobby; the god has been forgotten, with good reason perhaps. We know that among the most ruthless and relentless people in the history of mankind are theologians and politicians. For religious ideas and political aims they and their followers have been and still are prepared to murder and torture: wholeheartedly, single-mindedly – enthusiastically.

The thought I find so difficult to get away from is the terrible things human beings are able to do to others who are not gripped by the same ideas, by the same enthusiasm, and the damage they do to others, to themselves and ultimately also to ideas. Rejected, outcast, isolated, rejecting, casting out, isolating. The film re-activated memories in me of what I had experienced and seen myself in Berlin in those years; but also it made me look at what is happening now, here. I have heard crowds and seen them: I have also encountered personal reactions to Nazi ideology, and it was these personal views that were even more difficult to take, because at first it seemed unbelievable that people, individual people one had known all one's life, could – can – get so fanatically caught up in a cause or an ideology that negated every other aspect of life. I did not realise then that this is what happens when *archetypal* content breaks through. Now I know that the driving power of an activated archetype is immense, and that it will swamp any individual who has not acquired a certain degree of ego stability, a certain degree of maturity. I also know that an archetype can get a grasp on a whole nation. Most people long to belong to a group, to share a common aim and work for it in a togetherness which eliminates the need for individual decisions. This is a levelling down process and is inherent in the collective enthusiastic mood produced by an archetype. At that fateful time in Germany a hopeful belief in the golden age broke through: one thousand years of security, my morrow. The other, the enemy, the heretic in the form of un-belief, race, class, sections of society, would be, had to be got rid of by every and any means. Wholehearted devotion to a cause – enthusiasm!

Enthusiasm usually ends in disillusionment, whatever the cause, whatever the goal; no manic state goes on forever, a depression takes over sooner or later. When a collective condition is present and a general levelling down process has taken place, the individual is destroyed in the long run, though he might have experienced a kind of temporary enjoyment.

Today, we have feelings of anxiety and insecurity; inflation and disillusionment are with us; we are all affected by disturbing external happenings. We have the permissive society, we know about violence. What are our reactions? Will we be able to withstand the blandishments of unfailing remedies and of utopias? Have we learnt to understand human nature better, our own as well as that of others? How willing are we to admit our own inner cruelty and violence of which the outer is the mirror image? Convinced in our enthusiasm that there can and must be only one solution for everyone, do we refrain from looking for and finding convenient scapegoats who can be blamed for everything that has gone wrong? Do the old know this? Do the young know this?

These kinds of questions torture me. They are all connected with enthusiasm. They concern us collectively and personally; personally – here again I stumble. The word 'personal' reminds me too much of 'personne' no-one, nobody; of 'persona', the mask which can become such a fixture that the underlying reality is forgotten; of 'personally' meaning taking something personally, being hurt in one's vanity, being paranoid. Paranoia can render a person unable to learn from the experience of enthusiasm, unable to become aware of what is happening; whereas the hero who can disidentify and face implications to some extent, the hero who looks and wants to see, is the individual, someone aware of having an ego and having to make use of it. This process, the conscious confrontation of ego and non-ego contents of the unconscious, is a part of what Jung called individuation. In Kierkegaard's words it is to have the religious courage which springs from individual religious isolation. The possessing god is transformed into the inspiring god. Going back to *Cabaret*, in the film only two people were heroic in this sense: the man who found the courage to admit to himself and to others that he was a Jew, and the Jewish girl for whose love he does this and who herself had been willing to sacrifice her love for him, before she knew his truth.

For most Greeks the possessing and inspiring god was Apollo; he possessed the Pythia and used her as his mouthpiece, inspiring artists and scientists. His influence was civilising, moderating, giving ideal form; his opposite was the god Dionysos who inflamed and intoxicated, urging man on to break out of his boundaries. At the moment a wave of enthusiasm has caught hold of women who are fighting for their liberation, and in this context it is interesting that fairly recently a Zürich analyst, René Malamud, wrote a paper on the Amazons. His thesis is that they were inspired not by a god, but by a goddess: Artemis. Artemis was Apollo's twin sister; she was the first born, and it was she who helped her mother, Leto, to give birth to Apollo immediately after she herself had been born. However, for a long time her brother's light shone much more brightly than hers, but now Apollo's influence has waned and Artemis is regaining dignity and importance as the fitting symbol for modern woman, as well as for man. Artemis is appearing from the depths of the unconscious, inspiring and possessing, archetype of the Amazon of yore and of today. She presents an image of woman which is very different from that of the Great Mother Goddess usually projected on to women for good or for ill. Artemis is a virgin, at one with herself; inspired by her, modern woman strives to be herself, independent, self-contained, attempting to free herself from the shackles of convention and from the role ascribed to her in patriarchal society. Woman today resents being split into parts or playing just one role – 'being' nothing but daughter or wife or mother. She is fighting to be herself – as man is man, and then incidentally son, husband, father. This changing image is bringing confusion and conflict into the relationship between women and men, as man has to relate to his own inner image of woman in a new way too; he had to come to terms with an aspect of woman he has ignored in his inner world and not seen in external reality. Women and men have to review their attitude to one another; woman again may have the more demanding task: it is very difficult for her not to become a victim of and be possessed by and identified with a part of herself which she envies and despises at the same time.

Every god, every goddess, every archetype has benign and positive as well as destructive and negative aspects. Artemis is no exception; she is cruel and ruthless, she is not concerned with or interested in relationship. She is the huntress, the shooter of arrows; the bow and arrow symbolise her fiery passionate nature: she pursues her quarry relentlessly. She is goal-conscious, but she looks for new goals all the time as she roams restlessly through the woods. She neither needs nor wants relationship, and so her sexuality points to that of the unrelated adolescent. Promiscuity and compulsive sex are ersatz for relationship when cut off from feeling for whatever reason. Sexual and emotional dependence are all expressions of unrelatedness which is the negative aspect of virginity.

Bows and arrows do not refer only to sexuality.

> Bring me my bow of burning gold
> Bring me my arrows of desire
> Bring me my spear – O clouds unfold
> Bring me my chariot of fire
>
> I will not cease from mental fight
> Nor shall my sword sleep in my hand
> Till we have built Jerusalem
> In England's green and pleasant land.

Blake wrote this, Blake the seer, Blake the man who was ever open to the spirit. It was not the spirit of Artemis who inspired Blake. For most of us Artemis is a remote figure; we can only acknowledge intellectually that she is an archetype having a visible effect on men and women in our time, inspiring them with the necessary enthusiasm to adopt a new attitude and a new role. But though we may recognise her importance this should not blind us to the fact that her world is a world of narcissistic self-sufficiency. Artemis, the Greek goddess, lives in isolation and knows neither joy, nor sorrow, nor the glory of being human.

Blake was open to the spirit which stands behind Artemis, behind Apollo and behind Dionysos, the spirit which indwells in man and urges him on to search for God who is spirit: a search which drove man yesterday and drives him forward today. But even this search can have adolescent traits; Artemis roams through the woods looking for new goals, so people flit compulsively from one wonderful idea to another, never satisfied, never finding. They cannot find, because they search with such intensity outside themselves that they are unable to be still and to listen – to themselves. There is a gnostic myth in which Sophia – an emanation of the All-Highest quite a long way down along the line – is so intent on her search for knowledge of God that she is punished for her greed. She is condemned to wander over the earth for ever; at last, however, God is moved by her silent grief and her tears: He hides Himself within her: then she knew Love. Passion has been transformed into love, and the desire for outer knowledge into an inner realisation, into wisdom.

Enthusiasm is a fiery emotion, faith in a goal and hope of reaching it drive man forward. Fire brings light, consciousness and insight, but it also consumes and destroys. Enthusiasm is dangerous when allowed to rampage, when it is nothing but a compulsion;

but when an awareness dawns that even a compulsion may have meaning, it can be put to use. The transformation process called analysis/synthesis needs faith and hope as well as fire in both its aspects: fire and warmth to shed light, and fire to burn away old outworn attitudes. As a result there may be greater understanding of oneself and others, less rigidity, the forgiving of oneself and the healing of one's wounds, and the door to one's own creative powers may be opened. Some of you will know, some of you may remember that these are the things we ask for from the Holy Spirit – God who inspires and indwells in us.

However, there is one gift we hardly ever ask for, we are afraid of it and do not even realise that it is a gift; it is the gift of doubt, the gift of admitting paradox, of recognising the validity of the opposite side and the value hidden in it. Enrichment goes with this insight and pain.

A prayer that used to be said at High Mass seems to show the way in which the two opposite sides of fire, of inspiration, of enthusiasm and of ecstasy can be reconciled, in our hearts.

> *Domine, accende in me ignem tui amoris*
> *et flammam aeternae caritatis.*

> (O God, kindle in me the fire of your
> love, and the flame of eternal charity.)

5 LONELINESS

Loneliness is a feeling we experience, or a mood which overtakes us, or a state of being in which we live. We all know loneliness and the terrible feeling of being isolated, cut off from others, unable to make ourselves understood. We also know that these feelings well up from our depths, irrespective of whether we are alone, surrounded by people or, worst of all, when we are with someone we love. We may experience shame and guilt at our feelings of loneliness because we know that they are irrational and, if expressed, may be very hurtful. 'Loneliness is closer to me than my hands and feet'; this was said to me by a very beautiful woman who found it difficult to communicate through words. We experience loneliness when outer events force us to face that we are alone, that in fact there is no longer anyone there whom we can love and trust, and when we grieve in our hearts or are hurt in our vanity. This may last a little while or be a long time passing.

There have always been separation and death, sickness and old age. There has always been loneliness, but it is only comparatively recently that lonely people have become a social problem. In the not too distant past the family was a closely knit unit, and its various members were prepared to take responsibility for one another and give shelter to those who needed it. The wars, scientific discoveries and technological skills have wrought changes in the structure of society and our way of life at a bewildering speed. Some of the changes have been beneficial on one level, but they have also had unforeseen consequences. Thanks to improved medical knowledge we live longer, and this means more old people; our chances of survival at birth and in illness are greater, but this means more chronically ill and physically and mentally handicapped people. The family, on the other hand, has shrunk in size, and in general family ties have loosened. The old and the ailing who cannot live alone know that they are a burden to those they love and depend on, and they may realise that there is no room for them in any family home. When the day comes to leave for an institution they go, voicing their despair or in silent misery; no-one can accept emotionally that he or she is unwanted. Heartbreak on one side and guilt on the other destroy any relationship, isolate and increase feelings of loneliness; these emotions have become overt for all to see, whereas in former times they were usually more hidden or better concealed. The individuals concerned frequently attempt to repress their feelings as best they can; unwilling to look at the underlying significance of their fear and insecurity, they will blame society, or housing conditions, or the local council, and finally the state which promised us a rose garden and left us in a wilderness.

It is easy to sympathise and identify with sorrows and worries by which we ourselves feel threatened. It is much more difficult to understand that we are affected emotionally by the experiences of total strangers who have chosen to live in our midst. Immigrants escaping from persecution, famine or poverty, have come here in the hope of being able to build a better future for themselves and their children. Britain was to them the promised land, but very often they have been bitterly disillusioned. Refugees did not leave their countries willingly, they were driven into exile, fleeing from murder, terror and torture which are the recognised means of government by any form of dictatorship. Most refugees have lost everything that was once meaningful to them, and the majority carry in their hearts the horror of having had to leave loved ones to an uncertain fate, or knowing that they died in unimaginable agony. All these people know that they are unwanted and unwelcome, they are afraid and feel their right to exist is threatened. They are confused by strange customs and a foreign language which the older ones find difficult to learn. Withdrawal from their new environment is their response, and so they become ever more isolated, cut off and lonely people. The younger members, however, transmute disillusionment and disappointment into rebellion, aggression and violence; the resentment they bear us, their fears and their anxieties are influencing us more than we like to think.

Many attempts are made by members of official social services and by groups of voluntary workers to help lonely people; but in spite of endeavours to reach those in need, assistance is consistently rejected by some of those who seem to be suffering most. Tragedy and loss enter all our lives, but, for reasons we cannot yet fully explain, some people are more deeply affected by such experiences, particularly in early childhood. They seek and find refuge in an isolation which protects them from any form of relationship. Relationship is felt to be too great a danger, occasioning nothing but more and more hurt : isolation eventually turns into alienation. Estranged from life, alienated from others and from themselves they are imprisoned 'in the dark and the empty desolation' of their minds. This kind of loneliness is not only a social problem but a psychological one which needs specialised care. We are not all psychotic, but to some degree we are all neurotic; we all have to learn to disentangle our emotions, feelings and thoughts, and there are few signposts to guide us safely through our fear of reality to reality.

The great antidote to loneliness is relationship. In our white, Western, urban culture, relationships have become increasingly difficult though many theories are put forward about what they should be like and how they ought to be lived. A Frenchman who lived for some years in North Africa remarked that the most striking difference between the attitudes of the people there and those of Europeans was that in Europe people are much more related to things they possess and to abstract ideas than they are to human beings. It is certain that we are all very confused since our foundations have been shaken so badly and since the collective attitude to life and to values in life has changed so radically. The lifting of moral restrictions, the releasing of repressions and inhibitions in the sexual sphere, were expected to bring a fuller life to men and women alike, along with great individual happiness and a rewarding feeling of freedom. This has not happened; on the contrary, there is more emotional instability and insecurity in the permissive society, and more uncertainty in relationships than ever before. We are witnessing the tragic breakdown in the relationship between parents and their children, and their inability to communicate with one another. Relationships between parents and children have always been strained, but for the first time both the parents and the children are gripped by unconscious fears. The children as well as their parents are losers in this situation; both sides feel helpless and frightened by the split which has increased loneliness and despair. The problem is a collective one, but it can be tackled only by separating out from collectiveness, by individuals being willing to stand still and reflect on its significance.

Feelings of isolation are connected with the ego, but they go far beyond consciousness. At birth the cord through which our life is sustained for nine months is severed; we are quite literally cut off from the mother. It is perhaps from this moment that the archetypal fear of the void is activated which is later experienced through the ego in consciousness as separateness and loneliness. The feeling of loneliness is basically an expression of the existential fear of non-being, it is this that makes it so terrifying as it is connected with the instinct for survival long before the ego exists. The sense of identity develops slowly, the ego emerges gradually from unconsciousness, and it is at first – and often remains – weak and sensitive. When as children we become aware of our separateness, we are frightened of others who also make claims on the affection and attention of our parents; since we are unsure of our validity and value, we easily feel excluded, rejected and unwanted.

All adults remember incidents in their childhood in which dreadful things were done or said to them. In spite of the pain, fear and humiliation experienced, physical cruelty and violence are not necessarily the worst. Both for children and for adults, the deepest wounds are inflicted by lack of feeling and imaginative understanding. A young girl wrote to me: 'When I talk of aloneness I do not mean solitude, but isolation of spirit that I feel most keenly. It is this that constrains in me the impulse to give myself to people, that makes me ill at ease. My manner of experience sets me apart because for me it is incontestable and yet on the few occasions I have tried to communicate it, I have not been understood. And after these efforts I am exhausted, for I want dearly this thing to be authenticated which is in spite of me. But because the experience is not theirs, to speak of it is garrulous self-advertisement. I am more at ease with children than with these grown-ups who when they see what they do not comprehend imagine that one is showing off or getting at them.'

These thoughts are very typical, although few people can express themselves so clearly. In the long run it is this lack of concern for and unawareness of the individuality of the other human being which opens the abyss; it undermines any sense of validity and allows doubts about one's right to exist to creep into consciousness. Adults do this to children and to one another, but children also do this to adults and to each other, whether deliberately or unconsciously. We are all very unconscious and so preoccupied with our own feelings and affairs that we hardly ever realise how we affect others. Yet we are very conscious of and quick to react to the behaviour of others to ourselves.

In early life anger and resentment are means of defence and protection; later they do not altogether fulfil these functions. Feelings of indignation, however justified, may become a screen for unwillingness to explore our inner world and may prevent us from facing our terror of the void. Most people prefer to remain in a state of unconsciousness and take any kind of escape route which may present itself. Over-activity, noise, rush, rat-race, sex, drink, drugs, the shaping of illusory worlds or giving into orgies of destruction all serve as splendid excuses for keeping us safe from taking responsibility for our lives or knowing ourselves.

Knowing oneself means greater understanding of others and is inseparable from relationship and love. Having faced inner reality, we need fear it no longer, nor need we make impossible demands on ourselves or on others, nor continue to live in illusions and fantasies. 'No man is an island, entire of itself', yet in a sense we are islands separated from one another by our bodies and our skins, by the boundaries of our uniqueness. For split seconds we may be one with another in the height of the act of love, but immediately after we know again of our separateness. We feel this to be a tragedy – *post coitum animal triste* – and all long for containment and the connectedness which can be experienced only in the womb. To relate to another, to a thou, is to allow space to exist and to acknowledge it, sometimes sadly and sometimes joyfully. Rilke sums this idea up well in the following words written to a young man:

> But granted the consciousness that even between the closest friends there persist infinite distances, a wonderful living side by side can arise for them, if they succeed in loving the expanse between them which gives them the possibility of seeing one another in whole shape and before a great sky.

Every genius, every scientist or artist, every prophet has known and will know extreme loneliness. Ahead of their time, they speak a language which is not of time, and each experiences anguish. Some break under the burden of not being understood and of being mocked or reviled, while others bear it as part of the human situation. Jung knew extreme loneliness in his youth when he felt unable to tell his parents of his spiritual experiences, and again in old age when he knew that much of what he had attempted to communicate was being misunderstood or ignored. Yet he wrote, 'It is only separation, detachment and agonising confrontation of opposition that produces consciousness and understanding.'

I think there can be little doubt that we are living in an era which highly values violence and ugliness; this usually signifies the end of a cycle and of a civilisation. Expressed in terms of Hindu philosophy, we are living at the time when the cow stands on one leg. This also means that it is a time of transition and the dawning of the era in which the cow will again stand on four legs. It is a time of extreme tension, an unconscious collective attempt to give birth, aided by the striving of individuals towards consciousness and greater understanding.

Loneliness belongs to human life; it is part of our life. In the last resort fear of loneliness, aloneness and the void, is our fear of life and of death. We cannot change the facts of life, but we have been given hints about how we can transform our attitudes to them. The void can be experienced not just as a threat but as creative emptiness and the ground of being. We may be able to realise that our life is only possible when we are separate, cut off and on our own. Panic and fear of non-being may then be transformed into a deep experience of being, and being alone into being all-one.

ANALYTICAL PSYCHOLOGY AND
THE CHRISTIAN

6. JUNG AND RELIGION

Jung's interest in religion is well known; this in itself has puzzled many people, as it seems such a strange subject for a scientist of the twentieth century to be interested in. In fact it has aroused considerable negative feelings among the representatives of both science and religion. On the one hand his approach was that of a physician and specialist in nervous and mental diseases who wanted his medical colleagues to look at the avenues he had opened. On the other hand he also felt he was offering theologians psychological evidence for the validity of their intellectual formulations. In neither case did he meet with much acceptance.

Freud's position was at least clearly defined : religion was not a valid expression of the psyche, but an obsessional neurosis connected with the repression of infantile sexuality and incestuous wishes, while God was simply an extension of the personal parents. Freud thought that an adequate analysis could make an individual fully conscious of his illusions, and that thereafter he would be master of himself, independent of parent and God.

Many theologians and committed Christians have preferred this intransigent view of religion to Jung's more complex though equally consistent position. Freud might be accused of wilfully destroying religious faith and morals and of weakening individual responsibility by overstressing infantile traumata, but at least a Freudian analysis left spiritual matters out. Religious faith could then be left intact in a separate compartment.

To Jung, however, such a split, which left faith in an infantile state, was detrimental to the development of the whole man. The religious instinct which is present in everyone, though often repressed, needs to be recognised and fulfilled as a means of self-realisation. For this reason matters of the spirit have to be investigated as well as every other aspect of a patient's life.

Because Jung's attitude towards religion has been so misunderstood, it is important to see it in relation to his background and experience. Jung was the son of a Swiss Reformed clergyman, and eight of his uncles were also in the ministry. He was brought up in the atmosphere of a conventional manse where questions about religious matters were not encouraged. It was not necessary to think about one's beliefs, nor to understand them; all one needed was faith.

This attitude was impossible for Jung. From a very early age he was aware of his father's difficulties, his doubts and his way of repressing any thought that might not fit in with the accepted protestant teaching of scripture and the image of an all-loving, paternal, all-light God. He was shaken when he saw that neither his father nor his uncles, whom he deeply respected and liked, seemed to think about what they preached, worse still that it did not seem to mean anything to them, that they had not been touched in their hearts. The discouragement and repression of all questioning was deeply frustrating to Jung, and caused him much unhappiness, for, all his life, he wanted to know. Some children in similar circumstances would have thrown any form of belief over, labelling it as stupid or silly, believing themselves cleverer and more enlightened than their parents. Jung, however, continued to brood on these problems within himself.

Then, when he was about twelve, he was walking home from school on a brilliantly sunny day, passing the cathedral of Basle; he looked up into the sky and saw God sitting on his throne, and the spire of the cathedral sparkling in the sun. Suddenly a thought began to form in his mind – he could not allow it to come – he could not. He had a choking sensation, felt numbed and knew only that he must not go on thinking, because a terrible thing was coming, a thought he did not want to think, because it would be a frightful sin, a sin against the Holy Ghost. He did not dare tell his parents about it, for they would have been too upset. For three days and nights he was in agony of mind; again and again the forbidden thought tried to break through, though he did not yet know what it really was.

During the third night the crisis came; he thought how could it be that thoughts came that one did not want; where did they come from; surely if God was omnipotent and omniscient it must be He who put them there – just as He had arranged everything so that the first parents sinned: it had been His intention, just as it was His intention that he should be alone in his situation and seek and find out what it was that He wanted from him. Eventually the thought came that perhaps God was testing his obedience by imposing a task which incurred doing something against his moral judgment, against the teachings of his religion, and even against His own commandment, and perhaps God also wanted him to show courage. Again and again Jung tried to think it out, he always came to the same conclusion. So finally he allowed the terrible thought to come: God was sitting on His golden throne, high above the world, and from under the throne an enormous turd fell upon the sparkling new roof of the cathedral, shattering it and breaking the walls of the cathedral asunder. That was it; Jung felt an enormous indescribable relief. Instead of the expected damnation, grace had come upon him, and with it an unutterable bliss such as he had never known.

Questions however remained: Why did God befoul His own cathedral, or why did he force a helpless being into thinking something he did not want to think? This was a terrible thought – and also not to know what the will of God was. How did one know? With these questions and uncertainties came the dim understanding that 'God' could be terrible. Jung knew that he was in possession of a dark terrible secret which separated him for ever from his father, his family, and from all those who could listen to religious jargon without reflecting on it or questioning the statements made. Jung realised from then on how 'alone' he was; somehow he felt that having such a secret was shaming and sinister; it meant that one was 'different' yet, he needed to understand, to know, to experience. Later he came to appreciate the importance of the secret for individuation.

I have told this early experience of Jung's at some length because it shows the way his mind worked even when he was a boy. As an adult he was to ask the same kind of questions, he would continue to observe his own unconscious material with meticulous critical care. He did the same for his patients. Attempting to understand better and to know more he undertook his studies of religions and mythologies; he found in them similar images and symbols to those appearing in the dreams and fantasies – and experiences – of modern men and women. This convinced him that the concept of the unconscious containing only personal material that had been forgotten or repressed was too limited; it could neither describe nor explain phenomena of an altogether different kind which break through into consciousness. These came from another unconscious realm, the realm of a universal disposition in man which Jung called the collective unconscious or the inner reality.

The discovery of the collective unconscious was one of Jung's greatest contributions to depth psychology and a momentous one for religion as well. It is the realm of super-personal factors, or unconscious organisers of our ideas which Jung called the archetypes, a term he took from St Augustine, Dionysius the Areopagite and the Hermetica. We do not know their nature any more than we know the nature of the instincts, to which they are in many ways comparable, but we do know of the tremendous and overwhelming effect they have both on the individual and the group once they are activated. In the same way as new laws and new dimensions for the understanding of the universe had been discovered, so Jung uncovered layers and contents in the psyche, widening the concept of the psyche and adding a dimension.

Archetypes are a kind of pre-existent model of natural and spiritual phenomena which can be likened to biological patterns of behaviour. Inherent in human nature, they cannot be apprehended directly, but manifest themselves in an individual's life according to his innate disposition, personal experience and social environment. For example, certain situations which carry a powerful emotional charge – such as birth, love and death – are archetypal events and evoke archetypal responses that remain fairly constant in human experience.

Archetypal images originate in the central depths of our being and emerge as figures in dreams and fantasies or are incarnated for us by other people who carry our projections. Behind the personal patents there are the archetypal ones, benign or terrible, the Great Mother, the Great Father. Much of the power which parents exercise over their children derives from these archetypes. A child's experience with his parents colours his attitude towards mother and father figures in later life, towards authority and towards God. Other archetypes which are manifested in image and projection include the brother, the sister, the spouse and the child. All these figures play an important part in religious symbolism which can only be understood when their true nature has been apprehended in consciousness.

Concentrating exclusively on the importance of outer reality and the subject of consciousness (the ego), modern man forgot that his real centre would have to be the centre of his totality, of his unconscious as well as his conscious side. This centre, which Jung called the Self, is not static, however; it is a dynamic process from which the constant longing for completeness springs and in which wholeness and God are experienced. These longings and experiences are also archetypal phenomena, unconscious processes to which myths and religious dogmas give expression. When myths are retold as once they were, and religious dogmas are expressed, unconscious processes are awakened. It is in this way that religion becomes alive again and the relationship between the conscious and the unconscious is re-established.

Denial of the existence of this deep inner reality, its belittling or ridiculing, has produced a dissociation of the two parts, an alienation of man from his roots which Jung called the neurosis of our times. In fact opposites never unite at their own level: a third element is always required through which the two can come together. In the present context this third is the symbol. Symbols appear in our dreams from the centre of our being, as part of the ordering process which seems to emanate from that centre. They are the means of reconciliation between the conflicting sides of man's nature and between man and God. Thus reconciliation takes place when an individual discovers or re-discovers his religion – which has nothing to do with creed or belonging to a Church.

The Latin word *religio* derives from the verbs *relegere* or *religare*. *Relegere* means a careful and scrupulous observation of the numinous (the awe-inspiring presence of divine power); *religare* means to link back, bind back, reconnect. Both these definitions are of importance as they suggest two aspects of an active dynamic attitude of the ego towards psychic life, inner states, happenings in relation to external reality. To 'have religion' is therefore an attitude to life, to the whole of life; inner and outer.

Christian doctrine expresses for Western man the essence of inner experience, but it uses a language which has become meaningless to most people today. Dogma is no longer experienced, but believed in, or thrown overboard. When it is 'believed' in thoughtlessly, an individual subscribes to a creed. A creed is a systematised form of belief, enshrining dogmatic teachings carefully formulated by theologians, and it is enriched by ritual and outer observances.

Nowadays many people have nothing but negative feelings with regard to a creed – because they see in it only hypocrisy and being caught in rigid prejudice. Jung was ambivalent. On the one hand he called a creed a 'substitute for religion', on the other he attributed to it an important function. A creed is taught from above, one is told what to believe and this truth is absolute and may not be questioned; this makes direct experience very difficult if not impossible. So a creed stands in the way of spiritual development, and becomes a haven for those who shun responsibility, personal involvement, consciousness and maturity. However, a creed can act as a protection against the onslaughts of immediate experience for those whose ego-position is too weak to tolerate loss of certainties, or against the despair and confusion generated by feelings of isolation and the guilt of being a 'lone wolf'. A creed is a positive framework when the symbols of the church are alive and meaningful; when dogma, the creed is a personal experience. Belief, then, is faith, *pistis*, trust, and the opposites – religion and creed – are united.

One aspect of Christianity about which Jung was very concerned is the split that exists within it; the fact of which most Christians are unconscious is that the schism affects us, and that inasmuch as we proclaim to possess the whole, absolute truth, the more there is a split within us which has to be healed – a bridge has to be sought. We should all know by now what this aspect of Christian intolerance has done and is doing in the outside world; unfortunately there is as yet far too little insight into the fact that rigidity is also destructive to the inner world – in other words, that it causes neurosis.

Jung thought he had made his position quite clear regarding the question of belonging to a particular church; he therefore never ceased to be astonished when he received letters from well-meaning theologians, Catholic and Protestant, urging him to declare the absolute rightness of one church alone. His answer was: 'You seem to have very strange ideas about religion. Rightness is not a category that can be applied to religion anyway. Religion consists of psychic realities which one cannot say are right or wrong. Are lice or elephants right or wrong? It is enough that they exist. Religious statements are not opinions but facts that one can look at as a botanist at his plants. . . . Though I know little of Catholic doctrine, that little is enough to make it an inalienable possession for me. And I know so much about Protestantism that I could never give it up. With regard to this indecision I have consciously and deliberately decided for it. Since no man can serve two masters, I can submit neither to one creed nor to the other, but only to the one which stands above the conflict; I must be satisfied with being a Christian who finds himself in the same conflict as Christendom is in. I cannot disavow my brother who, in good faith and for reasons I cannot invalidate with a good conscience, is of a different opinion.' This attitude did not mean that he rejected or despised anyone who felt fulfilled in their church. He himself remained a member of the Swiss Reformed Church to the end of his life.

Jung was aware that many people were turning to the East, particularly to Indian spirituality, to get answers they felt Christianity was unable to give them. Jung had studied Indian and Chinese philosophy and religious systems and their impact on his thoughts had been considerable. It was quite clear to him that the whole spiritual outlook of the Chinese and Indian is based on what to us is profoundly unconscious. Had he been an Indian he would have been a Buddhist, he wrote – 'but for Western people Buddha settles our account too early and then it would go with us as it did when we European barbarians had that sudden and shattering collision with the ripest fruit of antiquity, Christianity – and so something in us has remained barbarian. This primitive in us who has been suppressed for so long must be given a chance to develop. It is no good building high up aloft, creating an edifice on top of the existing one. The existing one is rotten and we need new foundations; we must dig down to the primitive in us, for only out of the conflict between civilised man and the barbarian will there come what we need – a new experience of God.'

Jung's insistence on experience has made people diffident; they feel as if again something is expected from them which they cannot do. They do not realise that it is they themselves who shut doors because they have notions and expectations of what a religious experience should be like: often it is not recognised, it seems too insignificant, because of our negative attitude to ourselves. We cannot believe that we carry the God-image within ourselves. Not God, but the God-image.

Jung always said that he was unable to make any statement about God as this was the province of theology and metaphysics. He only knew of the God-image which appeared from within the psyche. It is experienced in waking life as well as in dreams; it is a deeply moving and mysterious experience which is accompanied by feelings of wholeness and fulfilment; it can be frightening and shattering : it is absolute. It is a psychic event which happens and which cannot be deliberately willed. In whatever way the God-image is experienced it is modified by the individual's conditioning and general outlook; in other words the ego plays a part in the phenomenon arising from the self. In the case of the boy Jung, for instance, 'it happened' in a kind of fantasy reinforced by thought. Such an experience by itself, however, is of little value; it has to be integrated into the fabric of the total personality. This is difficult; such an experience can be so numinous that one dreads to look at it with the eyes of consciousness, one would rather leave it in the twilight for fear of losing some of its strange quality.

When integrated, however, it is seen to be the realisation of our own inner truth. Then an individual may come to the knowledge of the laws peculiar to himself and find the bridge to the mother-earth of his individual instinct, instead of being lost in the arbitrary opinions of the conscious mind.

Nevertheless the ego, as dominant of the conscious mind, does have a central role in this work of individuation. In so far as it is willing to see, the ego is the mirror in which the unconscious becomes aware of its own face. It is the relatively constant personification of the unconscious meaning which is experienced in the rediscovery of the lost treasure of wholeness. It is often thought that this process should make us nicer than we are, but we can only become what we have always been, and this need not coincide with contemporary, collective standards of 'niceness'. Conversely the process will almost certainly involve the assimilation of much material that has been repressed into the unconscious owing precisely to collective disapproval. Take, for example, the case of a young Roman Catholic woman of about 22 : to the horror of her family she was suddenly refusing to go to Holy Communion, and declined to give a reason. When she herself had spoken to a priest she came to see me. After a while she was able to tell me that she could not go to Communion, because every time the Host touched her tongue she had an orgasm. This was for her utterly blasphemous, wicked and terrifying; because she regarded her body and its needs as wicked and terrifying whatever the cause. We worked through this; eventually she recognised that she had to link this experience to her total attitude of 'hate' for her body, and that from the centre of her being 'something' was pushing her to recognise the reality of her bodily needs as well as those of her spiritual side.

There is one more experience I want to mention. It is an experience a woman of about forty-five had in analysis. She was a Roman Catholic, she was fairly disturbed by material that was coming up from the unconscious, and so one day she went into a small church, just to be there and sit for a while. It was darkish: there were three altars; the High Altar in the middle and right and left of it side altars. She sat on the right hand side, and noticed that a priest was approaching the main altar, and was beginning quite obviously to say Mass. She was surprised as she did not think it was a time for Mass. She watched the priest, suddenly he turned round walking towards the altar-rails where she was, and she saw that it was Christ Himself who was offering her the Host. She took it; then He offered her the Chalice, she drew back, but it was offered to her again, and she knew that she had to drink. She said: it was bitter, bitter, bitter – and yet, He was there and it had to be. Then He was no longer there. In spite of the intense feeling that was connected with this experience, the woman wanted to look at it, understand its meaning so that it could become part of her life and be incorporated into her whole being; she did not want to keep it locked away in the attic of her mind as 'just an experience'.

It is not possible to give a full interpretation of this vision, but one important aspect is that according to this woman's religious background it was almost unbelievable that she was offered the chalice. The significance for her was the implied healing of a rift.

We are not accustomed to take our dreams, visions, fantasies seriously; for too long they have been considered to be 'nothing but silliness or illusions, even delusions'; Jung insisted on the eminently practical aspect of his findings with regard to the collective unconscious, still the archetypal nature of the God-image seems strange. Yet he made a new approach to the psyche possible, he opened a way for reason and feeling to come together from the psychological point of view by consciously paying attention to the psyche's manifestations; from the religious point of view by understanding the truth religious images convey through feeling being activated, and even to apprehend the real meaning of dogmatic statements: for instance the meaning of the Dogma of the Trinity, or the meaning of the Symbols of Transformation of the Mass. Jung had strong feelings about the *importance of dogma,* and conveyed this in his essays on these subjects. Theologians were disturbed by the notion of the indwelling God-image, particularly as Jung pointed again and again to the dark, terrible side of the deity. Traditionally, not only the transcendent God is pictured as nothing but light and all-good (omnipotent, and omniscient as well), but whenever the immanent God is mentioned He is spoken about as 'inner light' or 'grace'. Yet, the idea of God's dark side has existed always and has been expressed by man in his Holy Books : God is acclaimed as the Creator of the Universe, and as its Lord; He is Creator of all that exists, of Good and Evil as well as of all other pairs of opposites. As these ideas appeared from within man, they exist within him, and it is from those ideas that the image of God was formed. No scientist can prove the existence of God – that is metaphysics – but what a scientist did do was to prove the existence of the God-image in man in the collective psyche, and that this is an archetypal image of God. It follows that this archetypal image contains the light as well as the dark demonic side of the Creator. Particularly in Christianity this 'dark side' has been repressed. It was always emphasised in the Church's teaching that God's wrath was only visited on sinners; from Scripture we know that this is not so. Abraham and Job in the Old Testament, in the New Testament the Holy Innocents, the man born blind, or the death of Lazarus and the grief of his sisters are examples which spring to mind immediately.

This kind of knowledge is disquieting and so difficult to grasp that it is better ignored. It is easier to pretend that there is no darkness in God, but only in man. But in man only because of his own fault; sin, evil do not need to exist; they are only a mistake due to external circumstances or illness : evil is just an absence of good. And so evil is and remains unrecognised as a powerful reality in the nature of things, in the nature of God as in the nature of man – and no one is willing to take responsibility even for the evil which exists in oneself. Jung always opposed the concept of the *privatio boni* and had many long and impassioned discussions about it with the Dominican Father Victor White; equally Jung opposed the notion of man being totally bad, the carrier of all evil, which came in with the Reformation; blindness with regard to the consequences of the one tenet and the possible result on man seeing himself in such a negative light, did not seem to have struck theologians. This sorry attitude to the nature of man was reinforced by the psychological teaching that man depended entirely and totally on external circumstances and was determined by them. 'Call a man a name, and he will deserve it.'

People experience God in the peaceful beauty of nature or in its grandeur; very few would be able to do so in the horror of earthquake or avalanche : acts of God. Men of science are attempting to mitigate these natural catastrophes; man has not yet understood that eruptions and floodings from within his inner nature cause as much destruction as the outer ones, and that perhaps it might be within his potential, to look at and observe himself with the same kind of patience as the scientist does nature without.

Once upon a time there were scientists who did just that : the alchemists. They deliberately undertook the *opus contra naturam* the great work of uniting opposites and transforming the given basic material into the highest value. They knew of the dangers of this undertaking; the knowledge that their 'work' could be successful only *Deo Volente* was their protection against inflation and against being overwhelmed by their images; they knew also that intellectual knowledge by itself has little value : transformation implies insight, a recognition, seeing, realising on all levels and centres – which then perhaps is nearer to the idea of wisdom than of knowledge. This idea was expressed in their adage : *Rumpite libros ne corda vestra rumpantur.*

The *prima materia* with which the process of transformation is initiated has to be discovered individually by each alchemist. No one can be 'shown' or 'told'; one has to find it for oneself. The patient, bent on individuation also has to work through his basic darkness and unconsciousness. He may know neither about what that consists of, nor does he know what his highest value is. Is it God? What God? The golden calf? Mammon? His belly? In more modern terms : money, power, sex, or whatever else is the strongest motive power in one. 'Anything despotic and inescapable is in this sense God', Jung wrote, 'and it becomes absolute unless by an ethical decision freely chosen, one succeeds in building up against this natural phenomenon a position which is equally strong.' To undertake the analytical procedure is an ethical decision freely chosen. There are many similarities between the various stages in the alchemical process and those in depth psychology, including images and experiences. Of particular interest to Jung was the alchemists' concern with the figure of Christ. Christ and Anti-Christ; the Son of God and the Son of Man : the conflict between those two aspects, the problem of the crucifixion, the meaning of sacrifice and suffering, and of reconciliation and redemption.

This conflict and these problems are still with us in one form or another and have to be resolved. In his book *Aion* Jung had dealt with the psychology of Christianity in a detached and objective way. But his feelings were not so detached; suffering man, the suffering of Christ and the suffering of Job were all linked together in his mind. For a long time he hesitated to express his feelings, but finally he was unable to withstand the inner pressure and he wrote *Answer to Job*.

To some extent the book is autobiographical; Jung had suffered much, and from an early age he had been angry with God and unable to think of him as a kind and loving father. It was only as an old man, however, that he decided to write about his bitterness, his struggle, and the outcome of his conflict. But *Answer to Job* is much more than a personal account. He inscribed the book with the words, *Doleo tibi, frater mi*, David's lament for Jonathan. It is very much the work of Jung the therapist, caring for patients and concerned with human grief, who believed that the Book of Job has a special significance for the religious dilemma of modern man. The question of God's tragic contradictoriness is an experience charged with emotion which Jung had himself encountered. He hoped and expected to arouse thoughtfulness in his public without wishing to express any metaphysical or eternal truths. As it turned out, the book unleashed a storm of indignation.

Illness, failure, humiliation, tragic happenings are inflicted on Job; they are sent not by a loving Father God, but by a God who lets his dark son Satan have his way in order to see what Job's attitude will turn out to be. Job's friends tell him to repent of his sins – had he not sinned God would not punish him – Job rejects all such advice, because he cannot lie to his God. He has patience, he remains steadfast in his faith and holds on to his trust that hidden within the uncaring terrible God there is the advocate who will speak for him. Job the Jew exclaims 'I know that my Redeemer liveth.' The Redeemer is God's other side : His love and His wisdom. Job's insight into God's double nature, 'Lo, mine eyes have seen and mine ears have understood it', bring about the transformation in the divinity. But God has to atone for the sin He committed against man : He had to become man Himself to suffer the lot of man. God remembered wisdom. The wisdom of God is the feminine principle : Mary. In the second part of the *Answer to Job* Jung commented on the Dogma of Our Lady's Assumption. The feminine principle, the dark principle, the earth, wisdom, had joined God, Christ and the Spirit of Love. Jung saw Job as a prefiguration of Christ and at the same time as the man who stood up against the God whose force is beyond moral judgment; and by standing up keeping his integrity, transformed and humanised Him. The primitive angry self/God image confronted by an ego who knows of the Tree of the Knowledge of Good and Evil no longer needs to rampage. And then man can take responsibility for his own darkness and integrate it into his totality. When there is a dialogue between ego and self, the light and dark sides may come together – and this is the beginning of an inner liberation.

Jung affirmed that the indwelling God image was a paradox : archetypal good/evil and at the same time personal good/evil. And also in man there is an image of the One whose name we do not know. 'Even when man is enlightened he remains what he is and is never more than his own limited ego before the One who dwells in him, whose form has no knowable boundaries, who encompasses him on all sides, fathomless as the abyss of the earth and vast as the sky.'

This is the last sentence of *Answer to Job*, and well illustrates Jung's feelings. For those of us who were fortunate enough to see Jung in his home, the words will also be a reminder of the inscription over his front door :

Vocatus atque non vocatus, Deus adherit.
(Called or not called, God is always there.)

7 ALCHEMY

Alchemy is an art which has been forgotten, and represents an attitude of mind which has been neglected for about a century. Jung began to investigate the teachings and the symbolism of this gnostic system approximately fifty years ago when he was stimulated to do so through the strange unconscious material presented to him by a woman patient. He failed to see any meaning in the welter of alchemical literature until he discovered Greek and Latin texts. However, it seems that he bridged the gulf between alchemy and analytical psychology for the first time by means of a Chinese text which had been translated by Richard Wilhelm and which was published with Jung's comments as *The Secret of the Golden Flower*. Eventually Jung found in mediaeval alchemy a mode of thinking which he had hitherto only met in Indian philosophy, and he discovered in the despised, rejected material the great treasure which contains our own Western spiritual heritage.

Alchemy's heyday in Europe was in the Middle Ages up to the end of the seventeenth century, and though in the age of reason it was made an object of ridicule, alchemy continued to have a great influence on philosophy, religion, and literature until about the end of the eighteenth century.

Alchemy is a pre-Christian Gnostic system based on the idea of the perfectability of matter and on man's potential to attain self-realisation through self-knowledge. The whole process was called a *magnum opus* – a great work – and was considered to be an art. The Greek name for this art was *theurgy,* and the Arabic one was *alkimia.*

Theurgy means divine work, mystery or sacramental rite, and this word seems to have been used more particularly for the occult and magical aspects of the system. There were many true mystics among alchemists, and in theory there is a great difference between mysticism and magic. Yet for the mystic there is a danger of turning into a magician. This happens when personal power over nature is sought, and when the contemplation of inner things, which could lead to an inner transformation, slides into an endeavour to control the outer world and to bring about changes in external reality. Quite a few alchemists practised magic, as some kabbalists did, too, using formulae, names or numbers for various purposes, even for calling up spirits which might prove helpful in the furtherance of their work.

In the word *alkimia*, *al* is the Arabic definite article, but the origin of the word *kimia* is doubtful, some believe that it derives from an Arabic word meaning 'black land or earth', which would be a reference to Egypt; others hold that it is a Greek word whose meaning is 'to fuse or cast a metal'. It is significant, I think, that there is an ambiguity in the very name of a system whose main concern is to unite opposites.

Alchemy goes back to very ancient times, and from the beginning it developed along two parallel lines; there was the practical aspect, presumably starting with craftsmen who attempted to transmute base metals into common gold (*aurum vulgum*), and there was the speculative aspect practised by men whose desire was for self-perfection and whose aim was to make the non-common gold, the *aurum non vulgum*.

The mythical figure at the back of the esoteric teaching in the West is Hermes Trismegistus, that is, Hermes of the Threefold Crown. Hermes was a Greek god, and he was the messenger of the gods; he was the leader of souls, and he was a trickster; his Egyptian counterpart was the god Thoth, and his Roman, Mercurius. In alchemical lore he was also the grandson of Adam, and the builder of the Pyramids. One of the most famous texts, called the *Tabula Smaragdina* (Emerald Table), which contains all the basic alchemical teaching, is ascribed to him.

Alchemy flourished in Alexandria from about 140 BC and spread from there into European lands; in the Far East the art was practised in China. We do not know for certain whether Chinese thought was influenced from Alexandria, or whether Hellenistic and Egyptian philosophers were assimilating Chinese wisdom. The earliest relevant Chinese text we possess is an Imperial edict prohibiting gold-making, dated 140 BC; the inference that can be drawn from this is obviously that alchemical gold-making had been practised for some time. The oldest Western text is dated 144 BC but reference is made in it to earlier writings which have not come down to us.

Alchemical thought filtered into the Christian world through the Arabs and the Jews as a result of the Crusades. It was an Englishman, Robert of Leicester, who was the first to translate a text from the Arabic into Latin in the year AD 1144.

The basic belief of alchemists was the idea of the unity of the world and all that it contains. The vile and lower is not in essence different from the noble and higher, but different only in so far as in a mysterious way matter gathers to itself superfluities which can be removed without taking away or adding anything. The purpose of the operation was to make the stone, called the philosopher's stone, which was also the tincture and the elixir of life. This stone would transmute base metals into gold and secure its owner everlasting life. These ideas were shared by all alchemists, but at this point the ways of the men who wanted to make 'real' gold and those of the philosophers parted. For the latter the quest was a spiritual one; the ever-recurring phrase *aurum non vulgum* in their writings shows this clearly. The gold they were concerned with was equivalent to the 'Pearl of great price', and everlasting life meant for them life eternal in the sense of union with God.

Matter had to be transformed in order to free the treasure hidden and imprisoned in it. Man as body, and body as matter, correspond to one another, as the microcosm corresponds to the macrocosm, and in so far as the operation on matter was successful man himself would be cleansed, enlightened and atoned.

Alongside the belief in the basic unity of all things, the alchemists knew about the problem of the opposites in this world. There was no end to the various ways in which pairs of opposites were experienced: as sun and moon, as king and queen, as brother and sister, even as dog and bitch. Essentially, therefore, it was realised that the play and the clash between opposites in the entire universe could be best expressed by the symbol of the male and the female sexes. The supreme work of man and the main object of the opus was to achieve the goal of uniting these opposites in a mystical union, in the mystery of the *coniunctio oppositorum*.

The opposites constantly confronted the adept, who constantly attempted to see them and to describe them in one image, which can be done only in paradox. This challenges man in the modern world on his intellectual side and makes him feel uneasy, as he cannot understand the meaning or the sense of this attitude. It arouses a fear of being drawn into a psychosis or falling back into an infantile state in which one thing is the other and all is one in confusion; this fear will be the greater the more one is frightened of matrix, matter, mother.

Up to the sixteenth century in Europe, up to the tenth in China, the work of transmutation was done in the laboratory. The actual procedure varied greatly, but most alchemists agreed on principal points: base metals and substances were put into a vessel which had to be hermetically sealed so that there should be no leakage. This vessel was heated, gently and consistently so that the transformation could take place. Gently, because the art was a gracious art in which nothing could be hurried; consistently, because patience and perseverance were essential. Indeed, so wearisome and lengthy was the process that no one 'but a philosopher should dare undertake it'. Most alchemists were philosophers, scientists or physicians; among them were men whose names are familiar to us, such as Albert the Great, St Thomas Aquinas, Roger Bacon, Paracelsus Jacob Boehme, Goethe; others, such as Zosimos, Ripley and Dorneus have been rescued from oblivion through Jung, who made extensive use of their material. Among more recent alchemists who were fascinated by the occult side of the art are a Mr South and his daughter, Mrs Atwood, whereas the philosophical and symbolical sides seem to have been very real to Charles Williams.

Even if the process was successful it had to be repeated seven times – in honour of the planets – through all its many stages, and if there had been mistakes and failures, many times more. All through the great work the alchemists were sustained by their faith in a transpersonal power; and they were convinced that their endeavours could be crowned with success only by the grace of God.

The opus commenced with the attempt to find the *prima materia,* or as it was also called, the chaos. This was the first agony as the adept had to discover his own chaos; he could not rely on anything he had been told or on anything he might have read. The chaos was his own personal one, and the way to the goal lonely and occasionally dangerous. The primal stuff was then placed in a vessel and subjected to processes which differ according to the procedure chosen by the individual alchemist. Various stages follow marking the progress of the work, and these were called after particular colours appearing both in the vessel and in the dreams and fantasies of the alchemist. Colours were connected with the planets and these again with the destiny of man, and it is from this belief that they derived their importance. As the substances in the container changed, the adept literally saw the most curious forms and shapes of creatures, and he completely identified with them and all the transformations they underwent. This projection of contents of the collective unconscious which had been activated on to the material in the vessel was possible only because matter was still so very great a mystery to man in the Middle Ages. The alchemist knew what he was attempting to do, but he did not know what was happening and that he was caught up in a 'participation mystique'. The alchemists have described the entire process in great detail both in words and in pictures. Dealing with the first stage they show how the 'one' substance in the vessel splits into two, and the initial hermaphrodite is divided into king and queen, who are also brother and sister, and this brings with it much distress. This affliction is heightened into feelings of dissolution and of putrefaction when this king and queen embrace; it even leads to the darkness of death which, however, is necessary as otherwise the soul, which is the result of this incestuous union, could not be reborn and re-united with the body. Therefore this event is an indication that the secret tincture will appear eventually; yet because of the sombreness and painfulness of this time, the stage was called 'nigredo'.

The description given of the phenomena occurring at that stage are extraordinarily similar to those observed in analytical practice when the shadow is confronted. The shadow is experienced on many levels, but there comes a day when one's true basic darkness is illuminated and differentiated from superimposed feelings which only served to cloud one's vision, and which often made it exceedingly difficult to recognise and take responsibility for that which one also is. This is the beginning of self-knowledge. The alchemist was advised to pray most assiduously at this time; it was a dangerous situation in which he knew that he might be overwhelmed by demonic powers.

An interesting dream which can illustrate this stage was dreamt by a man in his mid-fifties, who is a chemist. 'I am pouring bromine into a vessel containing liquid air with a view to cooling and solidifying the element for storage; I do so too quickly, there is a sudden unexpected explosion, and I see, instead of a crystallised substance, phosphorus in front of me.'

The dreamer's comments were that bromine is a brown tear-producing element, and that the first part of the dream would be technically correct but the result was the opposite of his conscious intentions; also the coolness of liquid air could never actually turn into white heat. Phosphorus reminded him of matches. The dreamer tries to solidify brown, fearful feelings; being brown they are connected with faeces, the earth and therefore with the mother, also he wants to store them away. He pours the substance too quickly into the vessel containing liquid air. Liquid air is *aqua aeris* or *aqua spiritualis*, and this is synonymous with Mercurius. Mercurius as spirit is hermaphroditic and the principle of life which effects the union of male and female. In our case the element representing the mother (the bromine) unites too quickly with the life-principle, namely, the liquid air. The offspring of this dramatic union of mother and life is phosphorus. Phosphorus as light-bringer (matches) is Lucifer and has the same kind of extreme paradoxical qualities as Mercurius; he is the bringer of light as well as the bringer of darkness. Phosphorus is an aspect of sulphur and is a transforming substance: it carries much darkness, that is unconsciousness and shadow, yet it also contains the unconscious Self. Sulphur is the active solar substance which Dr Jung interprets psychologically to mean the 'driving force coming through into consciousness'. 'This driving force' (I quote Jung from the *Mysterium Coniunctionis*) 'manifests itself on the one hand as will, and on the other as "a being driven." "To be driven" is one of the greatest mysteries in human life : our will and reason may be crossed by something uncontrollable welling up from deep layers of the unconscious, and this may be destructive, but it can also be constructive, and an instinctive movement towards wholeness.' The dreamer's 'pouring too quickly' is a compulsive shadow manifestation, which at the same time has to be acknowledged as a being driven by the Self towards self-knowledge. The obvious sexual connotation of the dream bears on the dreamer's not having come to terms with his mother's lack of affection, and the state of his anima is well demonstrated by the abstract images all through the dream.

The albedo, the whitening, the silver or moon condition is also daybreak; it is then that the future synthesis in the form of the mandala can appear.

The alchemists experienced the mandala within themselves, and with this experience came the knowledge of the centre of the personality which Jung called the Self. At this stage the first positive *coniunctio* between king and queen comes about.

A very short dream may serve as an illustration for this stage: a woman of about 40 years of age dreamt that her left arm was covered with small wounds. A man whom she recognised as a healer put white ointment on them. She woke with a sense of release and well-being; the white ointment was the healing balm for wounds received in a relationship that had gone wrong, but also she experienced this man's action to be a fertilisation and therefore a promise for the future.

The next stage was called *cauda pavonis*, peacock's tail, because all the colours appear in it; the rainbow is connected with the idea of all the colours and with it the idea of a very special promise.

Goethe dreamt a lovely dream about this phase; he writes: 'I was in a large boat approaching the shore of an island covered with luxurious vegetation. Landing on the island I was struck by the great number of pheasants, whose beauty so impressed me that I bought as many as I could from the inhabitants. I then returned home in the boat.' In letters (December, 1786–87) he amplifies this dream: 'The birds were indeed pheasants, but they appeared to have long tail-feathers, spangled with coloured eyes like peacocks or rare birds of Paradise. There was a richness and profusion about these feathers, a glory of colour which filled the whole boat so that there was scarcely room for the oarsmen, and as the birds were arranged with their heads inward and their tails hanging over the gunwales, they formed a great circle of shimmering iridescence. The peacocks' eyes were of paramount importance and the pheasants acted as a screen for their blaze of colour.' Goethe was very moved by this dream; he took it to be a wonderful augury for things to come, and from his letters it seems as if this dream had made it possible for him to leave Weimar for Italy at a crucial period of his life.

Goethe had studied alchemy and he was a classical scholar, so he may have known that the pheasant is the Phasian Bird, named after the river Phasis up which the Argonauts had to row in order to reach the court of the king who owned the Golden Fleece. This hint at 'gold' connected with the pheasant is, however, only a cover up for the peacocks and for the promise contained in the colourful mandala they formed. There is an ancient teaching in which the four rivers running through Paradise correspond to the senses : one of them is connected with the eye; the eye is equated with the peacock's tail because of its many eyes, but also with the whole bird which was considered a symbol of enlightenment and of Holy Ghost. No wonder Goethe carried this dream within himself for a long time.

The final goal of the opus came in the *rubedo*, the reddening, the sunrise, the completion in which the final *hieros gamos*, the Royal Holy Marriage, takes place. No longer is there unconscious fusion and undifferentiated unity as symbolised by the hermaphrodite, but a conscious deliberate coming together of the opposites, a synthesis, the image of which is again the hermaphrodite : glorified body united with divine spirit.

Chinese alchemy developed very much on the lines I have been discussing. The idea of transformation and the change of one thing into its opposite always seems to have occupied the minds of Chinese philosophers, and the practice of alchemy led from Taoism to Laotse and finally to Zen Buddhism.

There are some interesting points of difference, however : the Chinese stressed the attitude towards the body far more than was ever done in the West with regard to posture, breathing and food whilst the opus was in progress, and they regarded the attainment of immortality as the principal object of the art. In the West, the folly and vanity of man appeared in his attempts to make 'common gold,' whereas in the East alchemy consisted in promoting longevity and indeed immortality to the individual in external reality.

An important idea in Chinese alchemy is that man's body is inhabited by the same gods as those which govern the physical universe. The sun and the moon are the left and the right eye between which Heavenly Consciousness has to be discovered. One of the most important deities connected with transformation and discovery was the 'Director of Destiny', who can be both a god or a goddess 'of the stove'. The goddess in particular is in charge of medicines and of cooking, and she is described as being a beautiful old woman clad in red garments with her hair done up in a knot on the top of her head. In Zen Buddhism there are no goddesses, but in their monasteries even today the monk who is in charge of the cooking holds a special position.

Earlier than in Europe, the sage in China knew that the elixir cannot be prepared in a furnace, but only inside his own body. The ingredients he needs are true lead and true mercury, not the vulgar materials. True lead is yang, the male principle; true mercury is yin, the female principle, and these two have to marry inside the stomach. This should happen when one is lying on one's couch just after midnight and/or just after the winter solstice, so that the mysterious pearl can be born. This is the new Self, enlightened and therefore immortal.

In the West there also exists the concept of the correspondence between the universe and man in the idea that the Creator first created the heavens and the earth, and finally man, 'the small heaven', who carries in himself images of the sky and of the stars. An example of this in literature is the mysterious figure of Makarie, the old wise woman in Goethe's *Wilhelm Meister*, who consciously carried the whole solar system in her body.

Jung stresses the importance of studying the alchemical writings for very practical reasons. No single person could collect material with such varied experience as those contained in the dreams and fantasies written down by men over the centuries. They are an invaluable source of information on the workings of the psyche of man. However, it has to be borne in mind that woman's psyche operates in a different way. Women alchemists are hardly ever mentioned. From the occult side we hear that Medea and Cleopatra were called theurgists; later on they might have been considered witches. One woman philosopher is named Hypatia. She was famous in Alexandria in the fifth century and immensely esteemed, but not so by Christian monks at whose instigation she was murdered.

The one woman who has left her mark on alchemy was Mary the Jewess, who according to legend was the sister of Moses. She is famous for having invented the double boiler (which in French is still called *bain-marie*), and for her axiom which Jung quotes frequently: one becomes two, two becomes three, and out of the third comes the One as the fourth. The importance of this axiom lies in the fact that the feminine principle of the number 2 is introduced and is interpolated in between the masculine numbers, and that both are united in one statement.

One of the great difficulties in the study of alchemical literature is that it is written in such an obscure and unintelligible way that it often seems to be nothing but nonsense in which no sense can be discovered. The question arose as to why the alchemists chose to express themselves in such a baffling manner and there seem to be several reasons. Many of the alchemists believed their knowledge to be holy gnosis, and therefore did not consider it fitting to pass it on to the uninitiated by clear instructions in writing. Their direct teaching was done by word of mouth and imparted only to carefully chosen disciples.

Another reason was that they wanted to shield themselves from the danger to life and limb coming from those who wished to possess gold in a very concrete way. These fears were justified; there are many stories about 'gold-makers' having been threatened, imprisoned and executed if they did not fulfil the expectations of their masters. The curious thing is that fairly frequently experiments were successful. Jung also thought that for the Christian alchemist there was the added danger of being denounced for heresy and having to suffer the hideous consequences of such an accusation. He shows in detail how the alchemical *magnum opus* differs from the *officium divinum* of the Mass for the Christian: the Christian opus is an *operari* in honour of God the Redeemer, undertaken by man who stands in need of redemption, whereas the alchemical opus is the labour of man the redeemer in the cause of the divine world soul slumbering in matter and awaiting her redemption. However, it seems that no alchemist was ever accused of heresy on the grounds of being an alchemist, and I was told by an eminent theologian that in a particular religious order the monks were forbidden to pay debts with alchemical gold, but were not otherwise restricted in practising the art.

It is true that alchemy carries the earth, body or shadow side of Christian teaching in so far as it is preoccupied with the transformation of matter; it is concerned with the lightening and glorifying of the body and the releasing of the soul from the dark prison it has fallen into. The shadow, of man and of the universe, its power and the power of the prince of darkness are experienced, but alongside is the knowledge of the light side, and of dark and light together forming a whole. Mercurius is at the heart of the alchemical opus, he represents the essence and he is the spirit who quickens and is present in everyone. Theoretically these views were acceptable to any believing Christian; for him God had descended into matter, into a woman's womb, thereby sanctifying it, yet matter was truly redeemed only when the divine soul was born from its dark prison into the world.

One of the most important images in alchemy which appears all through the process at every stage is the image of incest. We are aware of the incest wish mainly as a neurotic, morbid, concrete desire which can be uncovered in analytical work, and we also know of the incest taboo in most cultures. Yet what was forbidden to man was the prerogative of the gods. This means that an incestuous union may not take place externally, but that it has to happen, perhaps even should happen, in the inner reality. Incest in its positive aspect is a variant of the uroboros, which means being Self conscious, Self sufficient and contained. An incestuous attitude can obviously be destructive if it remains narcissistic and is lived in the form of infantile behaviour. In his book, *The Psychology of the Transference,* Jung writes that the most sublime feelings are contained in the incest situation, and also the most shameful. Once upon a time the alchemist worked through the various aspects of this union, and we have to do the same today.

The first incestuous union takes place in the nigredo and leads to the utter darkness of the grave; it is the time when we experience the pain, guilt and shame of our wishes on the personal plane. However, as we proceed on our way, we may understand that our desires are not only personal but transpersonal as well, and that, moreover, they may symbolise the means by which the separation and the breach of birth can be healed and atoned.

In Christian teaching the idea of incest is present, but hidden under a veil. Christ is the *sponsus,* the bridegroom, and the Church is the *sponsa,* the bride. But the Church is also Mary; Mary is the mother of God, and she is also God's daughter; she is His sister, too as Christ is Father, Son and Brother; the union between Christ and the Church takes place in heaven. We are members of the Church and we are also members of Christ, so if this union comes about in us it is achieved in the spirit, in 'heaven'. For the alchemist this marriage came about in the physical world in the image of the union of sun and moon.

The union in the spirit has taken place and so has the union in matter. We still need to know about the mystery of this holy marriage within the soul; then we have the three, and through this last union we get the fourth, namely, the enlightened individual who lives in time.

From the sixteenth century onwards it was realised in the West that the transformation of the inner man did not depend on the transmutation of matter outside. The adepts from then on wrote about three stages of mental union: the first step was to bring about the union between soul and spirit; and second the union between soul, spirit and body, and the goal of the last step was the union with the *unus mundus*. *Unus mundus* is the one world; the universe seen and experienced as one with soul and spirit and body is therefore the final experience of totality.

Jung describes these stages in his last great work, the *Mysterium Coniunctionis,* and he shows how the first corresponds approximately with analytical work proper. Comparatively few reach the second stage: it is the time when active imagination is practised, and one is able to enter into the psychic happenings actively and deliberately, consciously making decisions and ultimately taking full responsibility for one's total being. Stages and phases obviously overlap, and just as obviously they cannot ever be the same for anyone. Nevertheless, it is as well to try to understand what one is doing: analysis has to be gone through before a synthesis happens. The entire process has been called individuation by Dr Jung, and at the same time the goal of the process – if indeed one can ever speak of a goal – is also called individuation.

This terminology has brought about a certain amount of confusion, and has led to the idea that the analytical side of the work, with the emphasis on the personal unconscious, is neglected in analytical psychology for the sake of synthesis and the transpersonal side of the process. As in all such generalised statements there is an element of truth in this, but on the whole analytical psychologists are well aware of this particular pitfall. Psychoanalysts, on the other hand, are often accused of neglecting the synthesising aspect of the opus.

All methods and systems are but partial solutions. All knowledge acquired and held by the intellect only is bound to be incomplete. In Jewish mysticism true knowledge meant the realisation of a union, an embrace, a recognition in which inner and outer meet. The Upanishads teach that only an inferior kind of knowledge is attained through the study of books; this has to be discarded for the highest knowledge, which resides within the body and is attained by him who chooses. Chinese and European alchemy proclaim the same, thereby completing this circle of spiritual wisdom. Our mediaeval forefathers expressed their insight in a moving warning: *rumpite libros nec corda vestra rumpantur.* 'Break up the books lest your hearts be broken.' Our hearts will break in the endless search to find outside what can be discovered only within ourselves. The ultimate experience is enlightenment, is **Tao**, *samadhi, satori,* the Self, the peace that passeth all understanding. This can happen after many years of toil or in a split second.

This 'knowing', however, does not mean that all suffering is ended. In alchemical imagery, duality is still apparent in the ultimate union of king and queen in the final figure of the hermaphrodite. However much a personality is united within himself, he will remain aware of discord and conflict. The very particular importance of alchemy for the West is that it represents the one system which rejected 'doing' in favour of 'being'; in this it resembles Eastern modes. This is the exact opposite to the natural way of Western man, and so it is the necessary path for his completion and his wholeness. Analytical psychology today is the heir of alchemy; it is an attitude, a way of seeing, a recognition that whatever is darkest and vilest can be transformed into the highest value.

8 PSYCHOLOGICAL IMPLICATIONS OF THE DOGMA OF THE ASSUMPTION

Before discussing the psychological implications of the Dogma of the Assumption, I feel I should attempt to give a picture of Mary and the ways in which she has been thought of.

In the Gospels we hear of only a few incidents in her life, all of which are connected with the life of her Son. There are slightly detailed accounts of her during Christ's infancy, but only one incident during His boyhood is recounted. She is mentioned at the beginning of His ministry, and we catch a glimpse of her when She is particularly worried about Him shortly before His apprehension. We know that she stood at the foot of the Cross, and finally that she was in 'the upper room' praying and waiting with the Apostles.

Very few of Mary's words are recorded. She asks a question of the Angel, 'How can that be, since I know not man?' and she gives her assent: 'Behold the handmaid of the Lord; be it done unto me according to thy word'. Those words, *fiat mihi*, are the most glorious words ever spoken by woman. At the meeting with her cousin Elisabeth, Mary bursts out in a Canticle of praise (the Magnificat) 'because the Lord has regarded my humility'. Then there is a long silence till she asks another question, this time of her adolescent Son: 'My Son, why hast thou treated us so? Think what anguish of mind thy father and I have endured searching for thee'. His answer she keeps in her heart, as she does not understand it. There is another long silence. Then at the wedding-feast she goes and tells her Son a fact: 'They have no wine left'. That is all. Among some incidents which tradition has added are that she gave Luke the information he needed for the first chapters of his Gospel, and that she died when she was sixty-three.

From the start the Church held Mary in great veneration. Quite early on in the Eastern Church, she was referred to as *theotokos*, Mother of God. Four main feasts were kept in her honour, namely: her Nativity, the Annunciation, the Purification, and the feast of the day of her death, resurrection and assumption into heaven. This last feast was generally referred to as *the Dormitio*, the falling asleep. It was celebrated in the East before it spread to the West where we have known about it since the fifth century. At first it was kept on varying dates, but in the sixth century Pope Gregory the Great decreed that it should be kept on one day only, namely the 15th August.

During the following centuries, and even up to the present day, theologians and the most eminent fathers of the Church concerned themselves not only with Mary's personal life, but also with the actual meaning behind it. That is, Mary was considered not simply as an historical figure, but her life was regarded symbolically as a pattern of behaviour, and as a model for the possibilities of transformation which man carries in himself. Her 'being' was linked to prophesies in the Old Testament which foreshadowed her as part of God's plan for the redemption of mankind.

When we examine the liturgies for Mary's various feast-days, we find texts chosen from the Old Testament for the Epistle readings, and texts from the New Testament for the Gospel. In the liturgy of her Nativity, the Epistle is taken from Proverbs 8; in this we find the words: 'I was set up from eternity and of old before the world was made', and: 'When he prepared the heavens I was present', and again: 'I was with him forming all things'. The Gospel is taken from Matthew 1, 'the book of generation', in which four women are named as belonging to Mary's ancestry. These four female ancestors were: Tamar, who, disguised as a prostitute, seduced her father-in-law Judah; Rahab who was a professional harlot but saved the Israelite army; Ruth, not an Israelite, who by questionable means achieved what was fitting; and 'the wife of Uriah' (her name was Bathsheba) whom David desired so much that he sent her husband to his death.

The liturgy of her Assumption is puzzling. In the Epistle taken from Ecclesiasticus 24, Mary is spoken of as the cedar of Lebanon and as a cypress tree on Mount Sion. That is what we might expect. But the Gospel is Luke 10, the incident in Bethany in which Martha gets angry with her sister Mary. Martha is rebuked as being troubled about many things, and it is said of Mary that she has chosen the best part which will not be taken from her.

We know that texts were always chosen most carefully. It therefore seems permissible to assume that in some way a connection was seen between Mary and the two sisters. There are three women then, and surely Eve is the fourth. Eve, restless and active; Martha, restless and active. The two Marys, silent in ever-ready expectancy. Martha, in her eagerness to serve, overlooking 'the one thing'; her sister Mary 'choosing the best part', seeing the whole man, spirit and body. We know of her concern for the body, at one time experiencing it only on the 'natural' level; but once having met the spirit made flesh, lovingly concerned with His body. She is the only woman (except His Mother, of course) who is known to have touched His body, and she was the first person to whom He appeared in the body after the Resurrection.

Eve was created from man whilst he was asleep. She is man's mother. Yet, by her disobedience, by her disloyalty to the spirit, she made nature hostile to her kind, and brought death into the world, not the fruitful death of transformation, but death in the form of sterile dust. She too overlooked something. Mary, 'set up from eternity, forming all things with Him', co-operated with Him before time, and again co-operated with Him in time, allowing the Spirit to enter her womb, so that 'in time' she gave birth to the living word, gave flesh to the spirit.

That is one aspect. On another level we might say that Eve represents man's attempt towards greater consciousness, and the search for the ego, whereas Mary represents the Self and the Birth of the Self. Eve and Mary are our two mothers. Like sisters, they are each other's opposite side. Together they are for our Western civilisation the archetype of the Magna Mater, matter, earth.

We all know of archetypal Great Mother figures in other civilisations in whom the dark and the light are united, representing nature and earth in their double aspects of womb and tomb. The Indian goddess Kali is possibly the best example. The modern Indian mystic, Ramakrishna, had the following vision: he saw a beautiful woman entering his garden from the Ganges. She was with child. She gave birth and nursed the baby most tenderly, but after a few moments she changed into a horrible hag with a dreadful mouth and terrible teeth. She started to devour the baby, and when she had swallowed it she returned to the river. Ramakrishna knew that this woman had been Kali. He also knew that by this vision she had meant to teach him about the double aspect of nature, earth, mother, woman.

In Greece, as Professor Kerenyi has shown, Hecate the dark mother and Demeter the light are closely connected. This duality was joined by the Kore, the daughter or maiden, who represents 'elemental virginity', but is linked to the mother Demeter and so 'extends feminine consciousness both upwards and downwards' (Jung's words).

One of the most interesting Great Mother figures is the Aztec earth goddess, Tlazolteotl, whose name means 'eater of filth'. As mother of the gods she was worshipped extensively, and it was believed that by eating refuse she consumed the sins of mankind.

In Chinese philosophy, in the I-Ching, we get a completely abstract image of the feminine principle in a hexagram consisting of six broken lines representing earth. It is called the 'Receptive', and its four main characteristics are: 'yielding, devoted, moderate and correct'.

Turning back to Mary, we find united in her the unique concept of being both archetype and actual woman. She is not only the feminine principle 'forming all things', but Mary the actual woman who carries the darkness of woman in her blood. She incorporates it. By her reactions to the situations confronting her, she transforms the archetypal dark desire 'to be like God' into the acceptance and realisation of her body as the channel through which spirit is born into the world. Thereby she changes Eve's name; *mutans nomen Evae – Eva-Ave,* as she is greeted by the angel Gabriel.

The Christian tradition, based on Jewish thought, is a patriarchal one. This has meant that although the Magna Mater has always been there in the background, the Magnus Pater is in the foreground. Masculine values have been extolled and stressed almost to the exclusion of feminine ones. Woman in her earthly aspect became synonymous with evil – the seductress, the witch; woman's light side was projected into heaven as Mary. Mary became the spiritual anima, Mother Earth became darker and darker, and when during the Reformation Mary was removed from heaven, woman lost even that light side, and all nature, human nature, instinct and body became wholly evil.

During the time known as the emancipation, woman in her struggle towards greater consciousness began, in Jung's words, 'to make a concession to masculinity in establishing herself as an independent factor in the social world'. But she not only made a concession; driven by circumstances, she attempted to prove her 'equality' with man in the sense of sameness. So she identified with the man, with the male principle within herself, with the animus, and became possessed by him. Depreciating and devaluing her own feminine principle, her femininity got pushed into the shadow, and she became insecure, in constant fear of being overwhelmed by her 'feeling'. Living mainly the male side of herself, woman's relationships with man have become extraordinarily complicated. Having closed the door to 'feeling' on one level being frightened of her instinct, she has 'nothing to give' him. Every analyst knows about this tragic confusion and its manifestations: potential or actual homosexuality and frigidity. Man in turn has been affected by this tragedy. The dark devouring aspect of the anima – the woman within himself – is often so fearsome or awesome that woman becomes 'taboo' for him. Again every analyst knows this and knows the symptoms: potential or actual homosexuality and impotence.

During the nineteenth century Mary 'appeared' more often than she ever had before. It seems as if she wanted to draw attention to herself over and over again just at a time when woman became over-active and over-intellectual. It is as if she wanted to force us to remember what the 'whole' woman was. From this point of view her apparition in Lourdes was the most important. She appeared to Bernadette Soubirous, a young peasant-girl, standing in a cave quite near a spot believed to be haunted by evil spirits. She indicated a place and made the girl dig the earth with her hands, thereby bringing into the open a spring of healing water: healing from the earth, through woman. When Bernadette asked 'her beautiful lady' who she was, she received the answer: 'I am the Immaculate Conception'. By this Mary referred to her being before all time, 'forming all things with Him'. That is, the vision stressed the archetypal aspect of the feminine principle.

Mary as the feminine principle is a symbol of the Self for woman; for man she is the highest form of the anima. When Mary is viewed in this light it is clear that she is of utmost importance as a figure in dreams, fantasies or any other subconscious activity. Confrontation with the feminine principle happens at various stages of inner development and on different levels. We can and we do give this figure different names, but when we come to call it 'Mary' we are faced with great difficulties.

To some people it is sheer blasphemy to see Mary other than in white and light blue, untouchable, and unapproachable, and unaware of human suffering, sin or temptation. In others negative emotions are aroused at the mere thought of her; it makes them indignant that a mere human creature should have such privileges as being born without the stain of Original Sin (the Immaculate Conception); or *post partum virgo immaculata permansisti* being a virgin after having given birth (the Virgin Birth); or being assumed into heaven. These difficulties have to be overcome by non-Catholics and Catholics alike, in spite of the fact that for centuries Mary's mysteries have been meditated upon and her praises sung in the Catholic Church.

It is also true that Mary is alive in the hearts and minds of many, and that many see in her the 'joining-up', the at-onement, which is first an experience, and then becomes the task to be achieved within oneself. Psychologically this joining up and at-onement mean four things. Firstly, the acceptance of the body and instinctual nature as the basis and the vehicle for human experience, and its expression in outer reality as the Ego. Secondly, it means the experiencing of the true centre of the personality, of the Self, and thirdly, the at-onement of matter and spirit. The fourth implication is that woman, the feminine principle, is fulfilling its proper function, revealing itself as the complementary opposite of man and the male principle, and thereby is his equal.

The importance of these implications, it seems to me, cannot be overstressed, and the Dogma of the Assumption brings them all to the fore. In the official document, the 'Apostolic Constitution', the Dogma of the Assumption is defined as follows: 'that the Immaculate Mother of God, Mary ever Virgin, when the course of her earthly life was finished, was taken up body and soul into the Glory of Heaven'.

The significance of this dogma is the stress laid on Mary's humanity, that is on her womanhood and on her body. 'It is, moreover, reasonable and fitting that as a man's, so also a woman's, soul and body should have already attained everlasting glory in heaven', one passage in the document continues. However, in contradistinction to various modern ideologies in which the value of the individual human being is either queried or denied, the uniqueness of the individual personality is insisted upon by linking Mary's Assumption to the Resurrection of our bodies. This is expressed in the sentence: 'We hope that the exalted destiny of both our soul and body may in this striking manner be brought to the notice of all men'.

There is no split in Mary. There is at-onement and atonement. Mary is a woman. She is God's idea of woman, His feminine side. For the alchemists the Assumption was the end of the process, the completion of the 'Opus'. It meant the Mother-Virgin, *terra virgo*, is crowned, matter is redeemed and rehabilitated.

The Incarnation is the descent of spirit-man, thereby spiritualising matter, earth, woman. The Assumption is the ascent of woman, earth, matter, thereby materialising heaven.

The fourth has joined the Three.

According to the vision of a fourteenth-century Cistercian Abbot, Guillaume de Digulleville, Mary, Queen of Heaven, sits next to her King on a throne of brown crystal.

9 THE TREATMENT OF CATHOLIC PATIENTS

A high proportion of my patients are Roman Catholics, sent to me mostly by non-Catholic colleagues and several priests. They all know that I am Roman Catholic myself, having invariably been told by whoever referred them to me. They always express relief at being able to talk to someone of their own faith – even if they are what is commonly called non-practising or lapsed. Catholics are a minority group in Britain, and in predominantly Protestant countries they were often feared and even attacked at one time. They are, in fact, still 'the Papists' who feel sure that their views and beliefs will be questioned. Not all Catholics think alike, however, nor do they all believe the same thing. Quite apart from individual distinctions, Latin people brought up in a predominantly Catholic climate tend to be much less tense than their British counterparts. Most Catholics, though, find it difficult to speak to non-Catholics about matters pertaining to faith, and this results in a misleading impression of complete solidarity. The reluctance to confide in non-Catholics is probably partly attributable to a fear of seeming disloyal to the church. Catholics also fear that they will not be fully understood or that they might be called upon to defend positions which they themselves find partially or wholly indefensible. There is, too, the suspicion that a non-Catholic analyst will have no knowledge of the teachings and customs of Catholicism and will automatically react hostilely towards anyone who has.

While there is some paranoia in these suppositions, there is also some truth in them. Even Jung's understanding of the Catholic mentality was clouded by his Protestant background and upbringing, despite his tremendous feeling for everything pertaining to dogma and the spiritual. He made several remarks which affected analysis of Catholics in a general way and which may have had a bearing on treatment. The first of these remarks I should like to take up is one Jung made in *Psychotherapists or Clergy* : 'Many hundreds of patients have passed through my hands, the greater number being Protestants, a lesser number Jews, and not more than five or six believing Catholics.'

The word 'believing' is a mistranslation of the German term actually used by Jung; 'practising' would be a more precise translation, and this is a technical term. It means that a person is fulfilling his religious obligations by going to Mass on Sundays, and to Confession and Communion at least once a year at Easter time. Furthermore there are customs such as fasting or abstaining from meat on certain days, though many of the practices that used to be observed have been modified or abolished in recent years. A 'believing' person is someone who believes in the teachings of the church, but who for some reason does not or cannot receive the Sacraments though he may go to Mass and observe the customs. Most Catholics do, yet no-one asks what their inner attitudes and feelings really are. Through the years I have never met anyone who does not suffer from doubts, who does not have difficulty with at least some aspect of the faith, nor anyone who believes everything he or she has been taught. But many people – priests and nuns among them – hope that if they adhere to the outer rules, inner conflicts will be resolved. And so they hang on rigidly, sometimes fanatically, often in great distress of mind.

It is false to assume that practising Catholics are less neurotic than their non-practising or non-Catholic brethren. The fact that comparatively few practising Catholics have presented themselves for analysis might endorse such an assumption, but it should have aroused concern and led to an investigation of the reasons for this phenomenon. In an article in *New Blackfriars,* Dr Dominian remarks that several priests warned him against taking up psychiatry, considering it a potential danger to his faith. Though I did not have a similar experience, I well knew the whispering campaigns against analytical treatment that were raging among lay people as well as some members of the clergy. These people had one idea firmly fixed in their minds – that analysts were bent on 'taking their faith away'. I heard the phrase often, usually from mothers who feared for their children or from people who had already lost their faith. Such remarks can make those in need of psychological help even more reluctant to expose their doubts and failures of faith. So Catholics have tended to avoid the consulting

room, and usually only those of exceptional courage or those in a stage of despair or near-breakdown have come.

Another remark of Jung's which I would like to mention appears in *Psychology and Religion* : 'Creed replaces immediate experience by a choice of suitable symbols, the Roman Catholic Church maintains these by her indisputable authority; this defends people and shields them against immediate religious experience. If a patient is a Roman Catholic I invariably advise him to confess and commune as immediate experience might be too much for him.' Jung obviously did not realise how harmful such advice could be, particularly if it was taken as a result of the transference, and I wonder how often he actually gave it.

Confession and Communion are Sacraments – the Sacrament of Penance and the Sacrament of the Eucharist – they are not simply symbols. The priest in the confessional is the human ear through which one speaks to God, and on the whole people will choose confession fairly carefully. Confessions made by an individual and the formula of absolution spoken by the priest are not merely symbolic acts, they are experienced as realities. The Host, after having been consecrated by a priest, is the Real Presence, the body and the blood of Christ. The question of 'is', 'symbolises' or 'represents' regarding the piece of bread or wafer given at Communion is one of the basic ecclesiastical controversies. However, it is this hidden reality – this 'is' behind a veil – which means so much to the average Catholic and which is more esssential to his being than is generally realised.

Father Victor White was the first priest in England to advocate analytical psychology, and he did much to allay the fears of clergy and laity alike. Jung, on the other hand, wrote that his desire for co-operation with a theologian had now been fulfilled to an extent he had not thought possible. Father Victor's success in this role of mediator was due mainly to the clarity with which he distinguished between the role or function of priest and that of analyst. Jung had called one stage in the analytical process 'confession', which gave rise to misunderstandings such as that analysis and confession were more or less the same thing and that analyst and priest had more or less identical functions. Father Victor made it clear that the relationship between analyst and patient, the material dealt with and the analyst's attitude both to that material and the patient, differ considerably from the role of the priest in the confessional.

When an individual goes to Confession his act indicates – in theory at least – that he is sorry for what he had done or neglected to do, that he is penitent and wishes to make amends and seek forgiveness. The confessor (bound to believe what is said since lying to God is unthinkable) judges what he is told and pronounces absolution after having given a suitable penance.

It very much depends on the individual, of course, whether confession will help him to recognise his shadow-side and enable him to face and deal with it. He knows that it is through grace he will be able to do this, and through grace he will know of 'having been forgiven'. At that moment he will forgive himself. Several patients have told me that they experienced something like this when the words of absolution were spoken, though obviously not all confessions are dramatic. For many people confession is a terrible ordeal, particularly when they have to acknowledge acts they find shameful or humiliating – masturbation, for instance. Nowadays most priests are careful to establish whether such a problem is a deliberate act or a compulsion, and will often advise psychological help if they feel neurotic symptoms are present. The trouble with confession can be that an individual may know that he is going for moralistic or legalistic reasons, from habit or through superstitious fear. At the same time he may not feel he has done wrong, and may not understand why sexual activities are so emphasised that matters which seem graver to him somehow get lost. Such matters as envy, jealousy and unkindness at home and work are often bundled together as 'lack of charity'. And no-one can repent or have a change of heart if they do not feel or understand that they have done wrong. It is of much greater importance to point this out to a patient than to encourage him to continue a practice which cannot have any meaning for him. If an analyst simply advises a patient to go to Confession and Communion, the patient may well remain stuck in the infantile position where he was made to say sorry when he was not. He could then feel he is being forced to do things against which he may be rebelling. Then, indeed, such a state of conflict will effectively block any direct experience.

Patients seldom talk about their religion as such; they do so only when there is some major conscious problem. Born Catholics take many things for granted and often have not really thought about the implications or the meaning of dogmatic and doctrinal statements. When, in the course of analysis, doubts and questions break through, old answers are no longer satisfactory and conflict arises. (This may come to light through dreams; one such dream is of the patient's being back in his monastic school with everything looking dilapidated when suddenly a new path is seen leading outwards.) For converts there are different problems; they may find themselves in turmoil when the faith for which they struggled, does not resolve all their problems or protect them from conflict. Sometimes, there seems to be such a good external adjustment that only after long and arduous probing, the deepest doubt is uncovered.

It is most difficult to find the infantile superstitious level which a person is vaguely ashamed of, wants to ignore and at the same time hold on to. Some people prefer to stay in a passive, unreflecting condition, relying on a kind of magic; others were taught their religion badly, and they remain where they are because they confuse childishness with childlikeness, and remaining a child with being like a child. This lack of inner participation, or moral and intellectual discrimination, has to be tackled. Defences may have to be broken down slowly, but childhood faith has to be lost before a new and living faith can emerge. That is why I am pleased if I am told by a patient early that he has lost his 'faith'. It is a mistake, however, to assume that what he has lost is his 'faith'; he has lost his beliefs. Unless one knows the depths into which faith goes, underlying the superficial layers of infantile attitudes, and how it is connected with the fabric of the whole individual being, an analyst can make the mistake of thinking that everything has been done when the childish neurotic aspects of religion have been removed.

Quite a number of people who came to see me for further treatment knew that they had been greatly helped by their first analysts, yet also knew that there were regions that had never been touched. Material they had brought was brushed aside, and their own feelings about it ignored. This obviously interfered with the transference situation, led to conscious or unconscious resistances, a holding back of dreams, fantasies, thoughts and experiences. Apart from the patient covering up the apprehensions felt at his analyst taking actions lightly which seem to him to be sinful, there can be despair at being unable to speak about and to discuss the deepest things in oneself. This is all the more devastating to a patient as feelings in the church are of secondary importance; it does not matter if one feels like going to church, or saying one's prayers, one does it out of a sense of loyalty and inner discipline as a deliberate conscious action. Feeling therefore is neglected, and so it means much to a Catholic when his feelings, however muddled or neurotic they are, are taken seriously.

In 1958 Michael Fordham published a paper in *The Objective Psyche* called 'The Dark Night of the Soul', in which he refers to St John of the Cross and his experience of the soul as being divided into two parts: a spiritual and a sensual or sensitive part. The particular quotation Fordham uses makes an important point about even very spiritual exercises : 'when they are powerless to prevent it, impure acts and motions arise in the sensual part of the soul; this happens even when the spirit is deep in prayer, or taking part in the Sacrament of Penance or in the Eucharist'.

I was very interested when I read this, though at the time I did not foresee that I would have to deal with such psycho-sexual occurrences. But shortly after having read the paper a priest sent two women to see me, both of whom had had orgasms as soon as the Host touched their tongues at Communion. I think he knew about this though we did not discuss the matter. One woman was 25, born Catholic, unmarried; the other was in her middle forties, a convert, quite happily married with children, whose main neurotic symptom was claustrophobia. Both women were very disturbed, particularly as they were confused about how much their desire for Communion might be mixed up with their wish for another physical sensation. I thought of the 'causes' St John of the Cross mentions for such feelings, and the way he stresses their spontaneous nature. It is the delight of the senses which comes about at the same time as the delight of the spirit in God : 'Thus it happens that the soul is deep in prayer with God according to the spirit, and, on the other hand it is passively conscious, not without displeasure, of acts of the senses, which often happens in Communion'. The most sensible thing to do seemed to me to begin by stressing just this to the two women; I continued by attempting to clarify concrete sexual experiences and incestuous implications, particularly from the point of view of brother relationships – Christ is, after all, our Brother! In general I got both patients to speak about their physical fears and frustrations – the girl technically still a virgin, the woman afraid of the menopause.

At one time a great deal was written about the possibility of analyst and priest co-operating. Analysts said it depended on the priest, while priests said it depended on the analyst, and there is truth in both statements. A crucial aspect in the analysis of Catholics is the presence of the priest in the transference situation. The role the priest plays in the lives of ordinary people is difficult to define, particularly today when priests are consciously attempting to shed the heavy burden of archetypal projections placed on them. Within analysis 'the priest' can be an actual person: the man who sent the patient along, or a parish priest who has simply been told about the analysis. But unless they have some knowledge of analytical processes or have been analysed themselves, priests seldom fully realise the transference-countertransference problems which arise with regard to themselves. Frequently the person being analysed – the analysand – wants to talk to a priest in his role of Confessor, while at the same time dreading the Confessional. If a priest then asks too many questions, or allows the analysand to say too much about his treatment, such interviews may prove to be serious leakages and destroy the analytical relationship.

There are also unhelpful priests who are suspicious of analytical procedure and may try to warn a patient off; in some ways it is easier to deal with this type of man than with one who interferes unconsciously. Either a patient will react to overt disapproval – as he would to paternal criticism – by giving up analysis, or he will take it as a challenge and stay. The difficulty then, however, is that the priest becomes the recipient of the negative transference which should flow towards the analyst, and so a leakage problem remains.

Often there is no actual, outer priest but an inner one who is an extension of the personal father figure. Paternal qualities are projected onto him, especially in countries where priests are called 'father'. People who have been deprived of an actual father often speak with a kind of satisfaction about their many fathers. But when a priest becomes a love object for either men or women, and the hope of concrete fulfilment is expressed, one is moving in very deep waters. Incest is almost certainly implied, but so is a longing for union with God. In the female psyche one sometimes finds the figure of a nun, usually an elderly woman from the Convent at which the patient was at school. Such nun figures may be connected with a personal mother or may represent an old, outlived aspect of the Church in the patient herself; at other times the nun figures may even indicate the way to a more mature way of life.

These figures – priest and nun – appear frequently in dreams, and it is exceedingly important to pay attention to them as transformation of attitudes has to be effected from the levels they inhabit. The priest is the more potent figure since he is directly linked with the divinity whereas the nun is never identified with the Virgin.

Some of the problems related to priests will inevitably change in the future as the gulf between priest and laity diminishes. It may happen in time that even the priest's distinguishing dress and the title 'father' will disappear. Though changes taking place in the Church are affecting both priests and laity, it is not easy to foretell what the eventual effects will be. Many members of the clergy, as well as laymen, are bewildered by a revolution for which they are not ready or which impinges too much on introvert attitudes. And in contrast there are others who are impatient and angry because they feel that changes are not happening fast enough. Nevertheless, so long as essentials remain constant, an inner priest will continue to be a motivating factor in the inner reality.

So far I have emphasised only the difficulties of analysing Catholic patients since I think it important to show where particular danger spots exist. Obviously some people are more difficult to work with than others, and some are more disturbed than others. But I would also like to touch briefly on some factors which make work with Catholics no less rewarding and exciting than work with non-Catholics. When a Catholic drops his defences in relation to the analyst, for instance, and begins to look at himself seriously, he has an openness towards unconscious material and a readiness to listen that are quite remarkable. Once the transference has been established, it is easier to work through certain levels, and the distinction between the personal and the transpersonal is more quickly grasped.

Giving and receiving are problems which come up in every relationship and which can be very deep and disturbing. Through all stages of life the infant and the adult want not only to receive, but to give. In the Confessional a priest usually ends with, 'please pray for me'. One knows that the priest himself has to go to Confession and this underlines the fact that, despite many differences, there is equality between priest and penitent. This sense of equality is quite unlike any feeling one may have towards a parent or an analyst. One can pray for the priest – he has in fact asked for help. When analyst and patient live in the same parish they may meet at the Communion rails which has the effect of making the analyst less of a phantasy figure. But the really important thing is that the patient may realise that he in turn can do something for his analyst: he can pray for him and give his prayers to him. At the height of a negative transference this is unlikely to happen, but at other times it does. This gives the patient an assurance of his dignity and of his ability to do something for the parent figure.

I do not analyse only Roman Catholics; on the contrary, I have worked with members of every church here and in Scotland, and with patients who belong to no church but who are nevertheless deeply religious people. Had I not come across the doubts and problems which Roman Catholics have with their faith, I might have overlooked areas in the psyche and a dimension in those others who, in their different ways, are also seeking. In the end we all have the same problems; in Jung's words, 'childish dependence has to be sacrificed to begin with, and then an exclusive independence has to be relinquished'.

10 AN APPROACH TO PRAYER

Innumerable books on prayer exist, many of them handbooks from which one can learn about and be instructed in the science and art of prayer. I shall not deal with those things here, but with attitudes I have met with regard to prayer. Jung, for one, greatly valued prayer as a means of strengthening or keeping alive the meaningful relationship between the individual as lived by the ego and God. He wrote:

> I have thought much about prayer. It is very necessary because it makes the Beyond we conjecture and think about an immediate reality, and transposes us into the duality of the ego and the Dark Other. One hears oneself speaking and can no longer deny that one has addressed 'That'. The question then arises, 'What will become of Thee and of Me? Of the transcendental Thou and the immanent I?' The way of the unexpected opens, fearful and unavoidable, with hope of a propitious turn or a defiant, 'I will not perish under the will of God unless I myself will it too.' Then only, I feel, is God's will made perfect. Without me it is only his almighty will, a frightful fatality even in his grace, void of sight and hearing, void of knowledge for precisely that reason. I go together with it, an immensely weighty milligram without which God has made his world in vain.

As the extract implies, however, there are many difficulties connected with this attempt. The word 'prayer' tends to touch off our emotions; it may make us feel embarrassed, apprehensive, or even hostile since it may come very close – too close – to the innermost secrets of our hearts. The idea of prayer may bring up deeply hidden wounds and despair when we think of times we prayed in anguish for a chalice to be taken away, and it was not.

Our distress may have started in childhood when we were taught to pray and when we were told that prayers are always answered. We may have prayed and asked for a sunny day, or for mother's understanding, or father's safety, but it rained, and mother did not understand, and father was killed. Life went on : we grew up, and started to think, to doubt and to query the truths we had been taught, the validity of religious truths and the importance and place of prayer in our lives.

Prayer, it has been said, is 'the vital means of access to the seeker after God'. But, if God is, would it not be an insult to His omnipotence and omniscience to pray and ask for anything? And would it not be an insult to His majesty to approach Him without feeling like it? So we remain silent and maybe stop speaking to God altogether, as all too often our prayer has been unanswered. That is to say, our requests have not been granted. We feel that we have been rejected by God.

Yet, in spite of these feelings and doubts, there are many who will cling on with fear to superimposed ideas, performing religious duties more and more from a Persona level. Eventually such people are caught up in the collective aspect of some church, keeping the outer rules and regulations, paying mechanical lip-service. They will repress their doubts, be blind to their lack of understanding, and will therefore remain fundamentally untouched and cut off from the implications of the faith to which they are ostensibly subscribing. But there are also those who, disillusioned, reject everything in a mechanical way. They too will repress their doubts and be blind to their lack of understanding. Then there are those who have seen God and know Him by experience, and those whose thinking has brought them to deny Him.

Freud belonged to this latter group. To him religion was an illusion, the religious man a neurotic; to him the 'Father in Heaven' was nothing but a projected image of the personal parental figures of a psyche which had remained infantile. The aim of his therapy is to release man from this bondage, and by analysing his fixation on his personal father, to make him independent, thereby freeing him also from the 'delusion' of a transpersonal, transcendent being.

It is difficult to see how in such a system there could be room for the idea of prayer. Nevertheless, it is true that individual psychoanalysts have set out to separate Freud's psychological theories from his metaphysical outlook, and one can find amongst them people of religion. Indeed there are many religious people who prefer the Freudian attitude to the Jungian, as they believe it possible to keep the sufferings of neurotic man separate from his religious or spiritual life.

Jung's attitude is very different. He has never anywhere denied God, and he holds that the image of God as a psychological factor has influenced man everywhere since the beginning of time. A short summary of Jung's concept of the psyche illustrates what prayer can be when approached from the Jungian point of view.

For Jung the psyche is a whole. Its totality consists of pairs of opposites. These opposites complement one another, and our life consists in trying to keep them in balance. Any great one-sidedness inevitably leads to trouble; from within ourselves a constant attempt is made to rectify imbalance. This attempt shows itself frequently in 'neurotic symptoms', the dis-ease pointing to the error in attitude. From this point of view it can be said that the neurosis is purposeful since it constitutes a drive towards wholeness.

Body and soul, matter and spirit, the conscious and the unconscious, are some of the pairs of opposites. There will always be a tension between these opposites as tension is intrinsic to life. But tension may become too great and turn into bitter conflict when one side has been or is violated too severely. In our western civilization the neglected side is frequently the unconscious, the inner reality. This means too great an emphasis is put on the conscious side, on the outer reality, and on its centre, the ego.

We are born in a state of unconscious unity from which in the course of natural development consciousness emerges with the ego as its centre. Thereby a split between the realm of consciousness and the realm of unconsciousness, our matrix, comes about. We should consciously and deliberately pay attention to this vast other side of ourselves which not only contains our repressions and our reactions to personal experience during our lives, but which is the source of our existence and creativity.

If we neglect the inner reality we cut ourselves off from the riches and wisdom of all mankind; we will become barren and remain unaware of the hidden jewel within ourselves. This jewel is unique and exclusively ours; it is hidden in the real centre of our being and is what Jung has called the Self. In the Self all opposites are united. It embraces that deep realm common to all mankind in which archetypes and symbols are contained, and it includes the realm of consciousness and the ego with all the welter of wanted and unwanted happenings and experiences of our personal lives. To achieve a conscious and deliberate union of these opposites has always been considered a great work in which the ego has to co-operate.

Such union is the *hieros gamos* or the *coniunctio oppositorum*. It is *religare*, the binding back to the real centre, to that which in the beginning had to be differentiated. From this centre we can apprehend that our lives have meaning. It is from there, too, that the desire stems to become whole so that we may discover that what comes into our lives as happening – as 'fate' from the external world of reality, or else as 'symptoms' either physical or psychological from the internal world of reality – has purpose. The purpose is to learn to include instead of to exclude, to know about the light and the dark. 'To know' in the biblical sense, not as intellectual cognition, but as recognition in which our whole being is affected – our minds, our senses and our 'always having known'. This is an experience which occurs when we are close to the archetype of the Self, are touched by it in consciousness through some symbol of wholeness in dream or vision. This is the experience of the transpersonal power, the image of God within, which is utterly convincing and overwhelming.

Much confusion has arisen from this idea as many people believe that Jung equated God with the experience of the divine image within the Self. An extract from a letter of his clarifies this point: 'God himself has created the soul and its archetypes. We are dealing with what is the image of God and is numinous in God's own name. Trouble arises because my critics have not themselves experienced the numinous character of the archetype of the Self. By this experience we feel, in fact, as though touched by some divine power. Of course our symbols are not God. When I as a psychologist speak of God, I am speaking of a psychological image. Similarly, the Self is a psychological image of human wholeness, and it also is of something transcendental because it is indescribable and incomprehensible. We observe that both are expressed by identical symbols, or by symbols so alike as to be indistinguishable.'

Jung ends this letter: 'The best I can do is to have a divine image, and I am not the idiot to say that the image I behold in the mirror is my real, living Self.'

The image, however, is coloured and contaminated by the individual's experiences with his personal parents. If the individual remains fixed at this childish level, the mirror image of God in whose likeness we were created can neither develop not be transformed into that unique image latent in every single one of us. It is therefore of vital importance to get in touch with this image within, to confront it, look at it, even wrestle with it. As I quoted earlier, 'the vital means of access to the seeker after God is prayer'.

In so far, then, as we realise Grace, and the spark of being hidden within us, prayer is the deliberate attempt of the ego to get into touch with the indwelling, transpersonal image in the deep centre of ourselves. It is a turning inward and a conscious directing of libido towards the divine image. It is an attempt to make a bridge from the temporal conscious side, which is limited by space and time, to the unlimited eternal source and fountainhead. This directed attempt may then gather up and carry along the needs and clamourings of our personal longings, cravings or wants, coming to rest, entering from the deep within into the peace that passeth all understanding, in God.

As long as our image of God is too contaminated with childish feelings, our attitude to prayer may remain infantile. It seems to me that one of our great difficulties in being simple and childlike – as opposed to childish – in our approach to God is that most of us were unable to approach our parents spontaneously and without fear. Our 'feelings' may be those we felt in the presence of our parents, and therefore we do not wish to be reminded of them. 'Asking' then is an insult, or are we afraid of the answer? Very rarely does it dawn on us that we can speak to God as St Teresa did when she and her companions were thrown into an ice-cold river: 'Oh God, I am not surprised that you have so few friends'.

In his book, *Symbols of Transformation*, Jung comments on the following dream of Miss Miller: 'I had the impression as if I was going to receive a message. It seemed to me as if the words were repeated in me: Speak, Oh Lord, Thy handmaid is listening, open Thou Thyself mine ears'.

Jung contends that the biblical words contain a call, or a prayer, a concentration of the libido onto the image of God. The prayer refers to 1 Samuel 3, in which God calls Samuel three times; but Samuel believes it is Eli who is calling him, until Eli assures him that it is God, and that if God should call him again, Samuel should answer, 'Speak, Lord; for Thy servant heareth'. Miss Miller's situation differs from Samuel's, for in her dream she directs her desires – her libido – into the depths of the unconscious, and is anxiously awaiting God's call. Samuel, on the other hand, believes man to be calling him by his name whereas really God is speaking to him.

Like Samuel we may be called by our names and for a long time we may not hear. We may mistake the call from the depths for nothing but an external occurrence troubling our sleep. The call may be contained in our loneliness, our restlessness, our feelings of frustration and boredom, our grief and pain, success and failure, our joy and gladness, ecstasy and peace. Something is always calling us to hearken, something is always pursuing us to stay and stand still. 'Those strong feet that follow, follow after but with unhurrying chase, and unperturbed pace, deliberate speed, majestic instancy.'

In this way the whole circle is formed, the circle which goes out and comes in. Prayer is not only speaking and asking, but contemplating, waiting in silence, and listening. From our side and from the other. What will the answer be? A 'yes' or a 'no'? From either side.

God, the Self, the Logos in the unconscious (Gerhard Adler's term) are constantly working towards the goal of wholeness; greater than I, the 'yes' and the 'no' will be a *mysterium*. So, ultimately, is also our yes or no. Why, to what purpose are hearts hardened? Why do we not hear? Why do we not listen? I do not know. It is a *mysterium* which the human mind cannot understand. We can but recognize the ego's limitations and say as the Alchemists used to say, *Deo concedente*. God willing, God permitting.

In this way the ego places itself in the right relationship to the greater than I; no longer will the ego attempt to force issues by magic, no longer will the ego have the illusion of being master, but on the contrary will search and watch, and as far as possible willingly co-operate with the Greater to complete the pattern of its life.

Binding back, *religando* : through this attitude our split will be healed, and by virtue of this something towards the healing of the split in the world around us may be achieved.

Deo concedente : by work on ourselves, by prayer, by our attitude towards life which can be prayer.

11 FEAR, GUILT AND CONFESSION

Religious leaders and philosophers have always urged man to look at himself and know himself, as self-knowledge is essential for an understanding of the meaning of life and death. In our century depth-psychologists have devised methods of delving into our dark unknown inner world and getting us to realise some of the motives which drive us. Today it is stressed that such knowledge will improve our mental health and as a consequence our physical health as well, whereas in the past only the spiritual benefits ensuing from self-knowledge were emphasised. Self-knowledge is the basis for self-realisation, or individuation in Jung's terminology. Some people think of knowledge exclusively from an intellectual point of view, but in the present context knowledge signifies a kind of total knowledge of one's self – physical, spiritual, psychical, good and bad – which comes in a flash, then goes, and comes again. It is not a state, but a process of deepening insight which includes a greater understanding of one's fellow men, their weaknesses, conflicts and difficulties.

Most people have no particular wish for self-knowledge; in a vague way they are satisfied with themselves and do not see a need for or practical advantage in any of the hard work implied in the process of becoming more conscious. On the contrary, it is very tempting to remain unconscious in the Garden of Eden; there we do not take responsibility for our actions but can blame others, though we may have to bear the consequences of our conduct. It is obviously much easier to look at others – at one's friends or enemies, or better still at man in general, to indulge in fantasies and be stirred by incomprehension, wonderment or despair. In a curious way, however, we seem always to stand outside of whatever image we have, and we speak of people or of man as if we ourselves were made of quite different stuff. It is very sobering to realise that actually we belong to the same species and that in every individual existence, even our own, man is embodied and personified: man the creator, capable of the most sublime actions and thoughts, man the most destructive creature on earth, a mechanical robot, stuck in conditionings, non-conscious of his own cruelty and greed. This is what we all are, every single one of us.

Until the 1914 war it was assumed that man was a rational being who had become civilised. The war shattered such illusions, and over the decades man's barbaric cruelty has become more and more apparent, not only in his collective dealings with humanity, with creatures and with the earth itself, but in individual relationships. It was inevitable that this dark side had to break through at some stage, but perhaps because it had been neglected for so long, people became obsessed and possessed by it. The light and beautiful had been extolled in the past by artists in the widest sense of the word who saw goodness and harmony as the reigning principles in the universe. In our age it seems as if artists believe in and see nothing but disharmony, darkness and ugliness in the world and depravity in men's hearts. This despairing attitude is the counterpart and measure of the illusory world we lived in previously, and the danger lies in its one-sidedness which once again stands in the way of consciousness and reality.

Myths and fairy tales tell of innocent young princes and princesses cast out by a wicked step-mother who orders them to fulfil some impossible task. They usually find helpers in their quest who assist them in overcoming perils and trials and in performing dangerous feats so that in the end the treasure difficult to attain is theirs. The significance of these stories is that the innocent ones must learn to recognise the existence of the forces of evil and how to cope with them. It is only then that the treasure is found — the treasure which signifies wholeness. Wholeness means to confront the reality which is in opposition to one's ego ideal, and which is alive in the unconscious; the agony of self-completion consists in coming to terms with conflicting contents and assimilating them as best one can in the knowledge that they also belong to one's personality. This is in fact the process Jung called individuation or self-realisation.

There are also myths and fairy tales in which the hero is urged to take rotten leaves from the cave rather than the gold and jewels lying around in profusion, or to choose a lame, shaggy or three-legged horse rather than one of the beautiful sleek steeds in the stables. Here the significance is that the real treasure is hidden in that which we despise. We seem to have shuttled from one position to another, and this has made some people indifferent to important issues and unwilling to distinguish between good and evil. Others have fallen into despair, they are disillusioned and no longer believe in man's capacity to realise the everlasting great ideals. We forget the twofold character of existence, or else have never allowed this notion to cross the threshold of consciousness. Opposites exist; the unending strife between them is a condition of life itself and of individual life. Unless both sides are recognised and given their proper place there will be warfare which is experienced by the individual as neurosis.

Fear, guilt, shame and sin remind us of our badness; despite the fact that the concepts of guilt and sin are now considered outmoded and practically obscene, they still exist in the psyche alongside fear and shame. Fear has an object, one is afraid of someone or something, and this creates an emotional response; however slight or intense the reaction, the nervous system is affected. We share this emotion with all creatures, for it stems from the instinct of self-preservation and is a warning of impending danger. In man, however, fear has acquired further characteristics; it is not only his autonomous nervous system which reacts with physical symptoms, his cerebro-spinal nervous system is also implicated and psychic repercussions to the experience of fear can be long-lasting and damaging. Another difference between man and other creatures is that we are threatened most by our own kind; we tend to be more afraid of the behaviour and actions of other men than of anything else in this world.

The human mind is a permanent factory of fear which surrounds our lives. We anticipate and imagine dangers before they are actual, and we remember and cling to those which are past. Fear has always been deliberately fostered by those in authority; it was assumed that without the fear of punishment no child would be willing to learn or would grow into a responsible adult, and that without the fear of physical torture and mental anguish no-one would attain the Kingdom of Heaven. From the moment of birth demands are made on us and loss of love is a constant threat hanging over our heads. Later we come to dread the demands made on us from the outside world as we internalise them eventually and impose the shoulds and oughts on ourselves. We become afraid of failure, of incompetence and inferiority. We also become afraid of our emotions and our thoughts: we are not only jealous, we also want to kill; we are not only frustrated, we also want to break everything up; we do not only think about sex, we also want to explore ourselves and the bodies of our sisters or brothers or playmates. We live in fear of life and of death; we are afraid of being annihilated, of our identity being destroyed. And our fears become greater the more we are afraid of being afraid.

'Thus conscience does make cowards of us all; / And thus the native hue of resolution / Is sicklied o'er with the pale cast of thought.' Poor Hamlet. He spoke for all of us when we feel guilty of our fear and are spurred on to action by the terrifying thought that we might be found to be cowards. Our greatest fear is to be unmasked, exposing our smallness and inner ugliness, and then to be ridiculed, scorned and condemned. There is much fear and concealment in relationships; for we all go to great lengths to remain hidden even from loving eyes. It is right and natural that children should have secrets from their parents since this is one of the ways in which they can establish their separate identity; unfortunately, however, parents do not always see it that way. They either boast that their children have no secrets from them, or else they frighten their children into disclosure by making them feel guilty. Difficulties in one's own relationship with parents, added to the difficulties one may observe between the parents themselves, influence one's later relationships and one's readiness to look and be looked at. This is particularly so when falling in love and being in love transfigures the beloved person into a being who can do no wrong. Even then there may be lurking doubts, but they are pushed aside for fear of losing the magic of one's love. Trust takes a long time to build up even between two people who live together; it needs courage, patience, honesty and love to uncover that which one is most ashamed of; such trust is a rare achievement but it is the end of fear and the beginning of a new life.

The answer to fear is to acknowledge it, to look at it and to face the worst thing that could actually happen. Fear can then lose its blackmailing power over us as we are able to accept it for what it is. In the last verse of the Book of Proverbs where the purpose of the book is set out, we read, 'The fear of Yahweh is the beginning of knowledge; fools spurn wisdom and discipline.' It is obvious that fear in this context is different from the usual sense in which this word is used. The saying also seems to be contradicting St Augustine's 'Love God, and do as thou wilt'; or 'perfect love casteth out fear.'

Possibly the word 'awe' would be a more appropriate one; awe and even dread seem to convey more directly an attitude of humility, adoration, gratitude and praise when facing the divinity in one's mind; fear implies so much more an inclination to run away. But this is precisely what we do or want to do, yet we cannot ever run fast enough. We know that it is a terrible thing to fall into the hands of the living God, and we may try to escape, but in the end the Hound of Heaven gets us. We know that too. This may be a comforting thought in one way, but it is dreadfully frightening as long as we are unable to understand the meaning of events, happenings and encounters through which God speaks to us. It is not always easy to remember, in joy as well as in grief, that everything which comes into our life belongs to it, and that we can make use of all opportunities given to us to learn to be what we are. And so it is the fear of Yahweh which is the beginning of knowledge which ends in wisdom through acceptance of the discipline of the life He gave us.

·   ·   ·   ·   ·

There are as many ways of feeling guilty and as many reactions to guilt as there are individuals. We may feel guilty spontaneously, or we can be made to feel guilty; we may keep our guilt as a dark secret in our hearts, or we may have to share it compulsively and are driven to confess it. We suffer from our guilt, because being wrong or in the wrong belongs to our shadow side and ties up with everything we think of as being negative in ourselves. It frightens us to have failed and to have let ourselves down in our own eyes and in the eyes of others. Sometimes we are ashamed and full of remorse, and we may be afraid of having changed or damaged a relationship forever. The more insecure we are the more we always need to be right, and so we attempt to justify our actions to others, and can be so clever at it that often we succeed in repressing and hiding any guilt even from ourselves.

A certain degree of consciousness is needed to be able to experience guilt, for without it guilt feelings are a confused mass which are disturbing but unfocussed. In myth a sense of sin and guilt accompanies the breakthrough of consciousness; the bringers of light and fire are punished and condemned to eternal damnation because they also bring darkness and doubt, and conscience. Adam and Eve listened to the murmurings of instinct in the guise of the serpent, ate of the apple and became conscious of their bodies and their sexuality. When they heard God calling them, they wanted to hide themselves, covered their nakedness, were ashamed and felt guilty. They had lost their innocence and the state of unconscious wholeness; they had lost Paradise. Eating the Fruit of the Tree of Knowledge of Good and Evil had brought consciousness, the ability to differentiate and discriminate; as a consequence the problem of and conflict between opposites unfolded, and conscience and guilt emerged as an integral part of the psyche and the ego.

Adam and Eve are mankind, and their story is ours. Instinct, life itself, makes it impossible for us to remain in the womb of unconsciousness, it flings us into the dichotomy of this world, into the ambiguous experience of spirit and instinct, and of good and evil. The voice of the serpent is the compelling cry of instinct and the voice of God is the call of conscience reminding us that we owe obedience to the spirit which is the mysterious centre of our being and our creator. At the same time we have to face the paradox that disobedience and the Fall from Paradise became for man the *felix culpa*, the happy fault.

Conscience, *con-scientia*, is an inner voice, it is a special kind of inner knowledge; it is a value judgment with regard to what we ought to do, and a feeling about what we think we ourselves should be. From a psychological point of view it is important to know what kind of image we have of ourselves and how much the demands we make on ourselves correspond to or surpass those made on us by others, particularly by our parents. For Freud conscience is the equivalent of the super-ego, the patriarchal code of behaviour transmitted to and taken in by the individual during his lifetime. For Jung conscience belongs to the natural structure of the psyche, it is an archetypal function which represents the traditional moral code. It is obvious that the traditional voice of duty will be in conflict with the ego and the needs of today, but no-one can totally disregard convention and collective morality without in some measure losing his own humanity. When conscience speaks there is a war in the psyche. A choice has to be made and a decision has to be taken between what one considers to be right or wrong, or one may have to choose between two colliding duties. In either case emotions play their part and we have no real option but are driven compulsively in one or the other direction. Going against conscience calls up a kind of guilt such as we feel when disobeying our parents, or disregarding the collective values of our contemporaries. But when we listen to our conscience we may have an inkling that we are obeying not from virtue but from fear, and that in some way we are going against life. It is only when the ego is strong and steady enough to disidentify from either position that an individual can make a deliberate decision which is then an ethical one transcending the traditional moral code; he will carry whatever guilt there might be without being damaged by it.

The voice of conscience can be far more severe a judge than any external one; without invoking any mitigating circumstances it condemns and can make one believe that one is condemned for all eternity. Such feelings can grow to neurotic, even psychotic proportions in which one is haunted by guilt, convinced that one will never be forgiven by anyone and will never be able to forgive oneself. It is difficult to deal with such persecutory ideas, but it is an even more formidable task to get through to those who feel no guilt and apparently have no conscience. This is a dangerous sickness from which many seem to suffer today.

Owing to the archetypal system of conscience there is a dim awareness of ambivalent feelings long before the ego has been established. Infants have very strong emotions and express their pleasure, contentment and affection in unmistakable ways; but they show their frustrations, rages and attacking impulses just as clearly. Children masturbate whilst exploring their bodies, and their incestuous desires and fantasies have now become well known. Even though no overt punishment is meted out, infants and children know when they have offended and soon realise that sexual curiosity and gratification displeases when discovered. Much more serious as a source of guilt, however, is the oedipal situation. A universal condemnation of incest has existed for thousands of years and this taboo is an archetypal phenomenon; it causes immense emotional turmoil and is deeply repressed. Feelings of badness remain, however, and can create considerable damage in later life as they reinforce the corpus of unconscious guilt in the psyche. The pain can only be relieved when these feelings are brought into consciousness; for it is then possible to go beyond the personal concrete desire and to understand the transpersonal significance and meaning.

Feelings of guilt are not all sexual in origin or due to repression nor are they always neurotic: they are also connected with the side of man that is yearning for fulfilment in a spiritual sense, for wholeness. It is guilt and our conscience which make us aware of our shortcomings, and of the many ways in which we fail to reach or sustain quite moderate standards of relationships. We realise this when death intervenes, not only of a loved one, but also of friends and acquaintances, and we then accuse ourselves and wish we had been more loving and understanding. We do not know how badly we neglect ourselves and how murderous we are against ourselves; we kill parts of ourselves by ignoring them and by the desire to remain in Paradise without taking responsibility for who we are; we bury our talents. An elderly woman in great despair once said to me, 'I do not know why I feel so guilty all the time; I have done nothing wrong, I was a good daughter, a good wife and a good mother, what more could I have done?' This woman had got stuck in her goodness, but also blinded by it, repressing everything that had not fitted into her scheme of things. Her sexual needs had been fulfilled, but she had ignored and belittled as unimportant all her own aspirations and hopes. She had failed to pay attention to herself; allowing herself to drift into doing her duty and being used by others, she had thereby perpetuated a state of unreflected childish egotism and dependence on herself in her environment. The result was that she was feeling completely useless; in some respects she was right in thinking that she had missed out on something, for she had omitted to discover and to work out her individuality.

This happens to many of us, and sometimes we realise only very late that we were cowards, wanting a quiet life with as little pain as possible. The price for this is very high. At some point we have to gather up our courage and look at ourselves. In a loving relationship we may have to sacrifice our own hopes and wishes, and we may do so gladly and willingly or with grumbles and sadness. But if we know precisely what it is that we are doing, we will not suffer any psychic damage; we injure ourselves, however, by resisting consciousness. Guilt feelings and conscience are by no means nothing but neurotic and negative, for they can be of the greatest assistance by goading us towards greater consciousness and maturity.

All of us are easily convinced of our worthlessness; comparing ourselves with others will almost invariably lead to feelings of inferiority. We are on the defensive with regard to charity, we feel hopeless and faithless, and are very much aware of our many mistakes and faults. But even deeper feelings of guilt are expressed in remarks such as, 'I should not have been born', 'I ought not to exist'; these bitter words are spoken nowadays more frequently than one would like to hear. Even deeper one may find despair at the limits inflicted on the human being. Our body, our skin is the boundary which separates one from the other on the physical level; on the psychic level it is consciousness, it is the ego which is separate from any other ego, and on the spiritual level we are not God. So we believe we can overcome the deepest feelings of inadequacy, insufficiency and guilt by frantically displaying our power in every direction, for all to see in the outer world. This is not the answer. We have to turn inwards. Guilt can be forgiven. We have to learn to forgive ourselves; we have to learn to accept guilt as belonging to our humanity, and be willing to carry it. We are not omnipotent, nor are we omniscient. We cannot do everything we would like to have done, nor have everything we desired, nor can we be other than we are. Once we take responsibility for our life, for all our wrongness and badness and our rightness and goodness, we may ultimately be able to suffer guilt willingly and apprehend redemption by tasting the Fruit of the Tree of Life.

· · · ·

When we are very young and feel badly about something we have done, we may run to mother and confess to her without fear; we may get scolded a bit, but then we are forgiven and can be happy again. It does not take us long, however, to learn that confessions are often followed by unpleasant consequences. So we learn to conceal, to have guilty secrets and not to let on until we are found out. Secrets can be helpful on the other hand, as our separateness and a feeling for our identity can grow from them. But when we begin to have secrets from ourselves by repressing everything we believe to be unacceptable, we are in danger of partially destroying ourselves.

Concealment is the opposite of confession; our first secret is the end of an era and the beginning of a new period in our psychic development. We are no longer able to say spontaneously what we feel or what we have done; we become dimly aware that even genuine mistakes and genuinely not knowing may be followed by unfortunate results, if not punishment. We learn to curse ourselves for not knowing, for being wrong, for being stupid. We attribute these unhappy reactions to the personal mismanagement of our parents or other authority figures. Actually we should not blame them exclusively, it is nature which is not interested in ignorance, and life itself which makes one pay the penalty of unconsciousness. Attempts may be made to break through the walls we have built up, and we dare to do and say things to the consternation of those in our environment and of ourselves. But when we realise how isolated we are going to be unless we return to the fold and obey collective demands, we may lose courage and give in, repressing our feelings more and more in order to exist. Eventually we no longer know who or what we are; we wear a mask which hides us from others as well as from ourselves inasmuch as we identify with it by showing ourselves only as we think we ought to be. However brittle, empty and insecure we feel, we are far too frightened to look at what lies behind this mask by ourselves alone. This is the stuff a neurosis is made of and feeds on; it is only when the inner unrest produces physical or psychic symptoms that we agree to seek help and may begin to pay attention to our inner world.

The great discovery of depth-psychology was that the only effective answer to repression and concealment is their opposite – confession. Confession of one's sufferings, of painful experiences in one's early life, of one's lack of understanding of so many things, and also of one's feelings of helplessness and inferiority. Jung called this kind of confession the first stage of analysis as he saw in it a method of treatment and recognised its importance for a systematic verbal approach to buried material. We are enriched by doing this, for we find that it contains much of great value to us, and so we become strong enough to acknowledge our really dark, unbeautiful sides. The confessing itself, the saying things out loud in the presence of another, can be a distressing and humiliating experience, but it also brings with it feelings of tremendous relief.

The experience of feeling released, freed and cleansed is also made in many encounter-like groups in which confessions play an important part. Sophisticated techniques are used to get the participants quite quickly into a frame of mind which enables them to remove their protective masks and expose their emotions in front of the group, shedding all ego-respect. At the end of such a profound emotional experience participants find themselves surrounded and supported by the whole group. One generally expects to be acceptable to an analyst or a group leader, but the supporting reaction of the group to one's inner poverty and frailty seems a complete miracle. One realises with some shock that under the masks everyone is wearing there may be fear and envy and cynicism, but there is also understanding and compassion.

Confessions made under duress are obviously of no benefit to an individual. Neither are the unconscious confessions of those who, with loving care for detail, write or produce documentaries or plays in which every kind of sickening brutality and violence are shown, or in which the unhappiness of human relationships is dwelt on. Ostensibly this is done to give us a true picture of the state of our society, but one may seriously ask whether such spectacles are not in fact representations of personal unhappiness or revelations of secret, sadistic fantasies which relieve their authors of guilt feelings.

Long before confessions were discovered to be valuable in the treatment of neurosis, confession was practised in the Catholic Church. For Catholics confession is a sacrament, the Sacrament of Penance. In sacramental confession there are, of course, elements one does not find in the psychological situation, namely the notions of repentance, penance and absolution. One confesses one's sins, the wrongs one has done to others, to one's neighbours, to the community, to self and to God. It is actions, thoughts, and feelings that matter, not the psychological motivation underlying them. Confession of sin implies that one recognises what one has done, thought or felt as wrong; sin is a deliberate action and confession an act of free will. Compulsive action or unconscious behaviour are not sin. We cannot confess things of which we are unconscious, such as being deceitful and lying to ourselves and others. We do not commit actual murder, but we do not realise that we are killing any joy around us and destroying any kind of self-confidence; we may believe ourselves to be innocent of adultery though lusting after our neigbour's wife in our hearts. Self-examination may help us to detect areas of vindictiveness and of hypocrisy in ourselves, and, just as important, we may also discover parts which would want to change and transform such areas.

Confession presupposes that man is a sinner, but also that he is capable of taking responsibility for what he is and of turning away from his sin, not by himself, not by ego-will only, but with the help of God's grace. The Sacrament was instituted as a means of healing a troubled soul and providing an opportunity to speak to God about one's sorrow for having done damage. This sorrow is not only a feeling of remorse, but an act of will and a willingness to change one's attitude, to change one's heart and mind, and this is *metanoia* or repentance. The priest is the witness to this act of stripping; his role is to assess what one has said, to give spiritual advice and comfort, to impose a penance, and finally to pronounce the words of forgiveness in the name of God. The prayer of absolution puts the seal on one's reconciliation to the transcendent God, to the God-image within, and to one's self. Our sense of dignity is restored and we are newly able to rely on grace and the Holy Spirit; we are able, too, to forgive others and to have the courage to ask forgiveness for any hurt or damage we have caused.

There is no rule about how often one should go to confession; one is expected to go at least once a year, though during this century Catholics have been exhorted to go very much more frequently. Recently it was noticed that fewer people made use of the Sacrament, and the Church decided for very good reasons that the outer forms of the Sacrament should be modified. It was realised that the usual Saturday afternoon confessions had become an almost mechanical exercise. Far too little thought seemed to be given to preparation for the Sacrament; added to this was the fact that once in the confessional the priest was unable to give sufficient time to the individual, and the penitent himself was too aware of the people waiting outside for their turn. The time spent saying one's penance also seemed to be cut very short, for that too had become automatic. Furthermore, people had become much more uncertain about what they should be confessing. At one time practically everything connected with sex seemed to be considered the only truly sinful thing, so if one did not know what else to say there was always the possibility of recalling a sin with regard to sex. It is much more difficult if there were nothing of that kind to confess because even the lists of sins printed in the little books designed to help formulate one's thoughts did not always seem relevant to one's own situation. The tendency was, therefore, to lump everything together under the formula of having sinned against charity. The priest could not help one as much as he might have liked, for, apart from not being able to see one through the grille of the confessional, he usually did not know one.

Since Vatican II many changes have been introduced by the Church with regard to outer forms. Some of these changes were welcomed while others were severely criticised and even produced unhappiness and heartache. The use of the vernacular was not altogether popular owing to translations which were not liked, and it was felt that the need for silence and introversion during the celebration of Mass had been forgotten and ignored. It is only now, after several years, that the deep implications of the changes have become apparent even to those who were most critical. One of the most important is the emphasis on man's being a whole, so that we no longer ask God to heal our souls or be with our spirit, we simply ask to be healed or for his presence to be with the totality of our being, body, soul and spirit. The other far-reaching change is the emphasis placed on all of us belonging together as a family of brothers and sisters, as members of the mystical body of Christ, and on the idea that we affect one another by our actions and our attitudes.

For most Catholics confession is a duty which has to be performed from time to time for the sake of receiving Communion, the Sacrament of the Holy Eucharist. Strictly speaking confession is necessary only when a grave sin has been committed, but its value lies in the realisation of always needing forgiveness and of expressing one's goodwill, one's faith and hope. The idea that confession is the gateway to Communion is firmly implanted from early childhood; the greatest religious event in the life of a child is his first communion, and this is preceded by his first confession. The advisability of having sacramental confession for children is under discussion in many countries; in England the Hierarchy has come down on the side of continuing the practice. The counter-arguments are that a child of six or seven years of age is unable to understand the meaning of sin; to him it simply means having been naughty. It is also thought that the patterns of such early confessions are carried over into adult life and constitute a conditioning of which it is difficult to free oneself. In the Russian Orthodox Church a child of that age can receive Communion, but only much later is he allowed to confess.

Interestingly enough the new way of administering the Sacrament of Penance to individuals is very close to the manner in which confessions are heard in the Russian Orthodox Church. The priest and the penitent meet in a suitable part of the Church and need no longer use the confessional which separates them. An individual may then talk about the nature of his problems and the difficulties he finds himself in. The priest is therefore in a much better position to judge the whole situation and so really to help in making the confession a meaningful experience.

In a more collective way penitential services are now provided which should be helpful to many people whose need is to feel less alone in their sorrow and their desire to be forgiven. After having expressed this together with others, individuals are able to ask for absolution in private if they wish; the service ends with communal thanksgiving. A much greater sense of being included and belonging is achieved in this way which is important at a time when so many feel excluded and isolated. Whoever shaped these new forms must have been inspired by the Holy Spirit, for they do away with misgivings and resistances, and may fulfil the needs of many who have gone away hungry in the past.

In Jung's terminology, the first stage in analysis is confession which is followed by elucidation, education and finally transformation. These stages do not necessarily refer to linear time, neither does progress take place in a straight line, the image is rather that of the spiral. In a single analytical session one may get the feeling of having found the key to the door of one's prison, only to find that one has lost it again after a short while. This is an experience which one gets to know quite well, but one plods on because one realises that the components of the psyche have to be analysed and scrutinized. The light of understanding has to be brought into the darkness of disorder, and then eventually a synthesis, in the shape of a different pattern, can emerge into consciousness. This is the inner transformation which shows that one no longer splits off parts of oneself, pretending they do not exist because one is so horrified and ashamed of them. Jung called this whole procedure the process of individuation or self-realisation which is set in motion through analysis.

The process of unfolding and developing one's personality goes on all through life, but, when it gets stuck, help is needed to get it going again. In analysis we ask the question 'Why did this happen?' which is going back in time to childhood and infancy, and to the complex which stands in our way. When we have learnt to differentiate between ourselves and others, and are more secure in the value of our own being, we begin to withdraw projections and to have reactions and emotions instead of being possessed by them. Then we may ask the question. 'What did this happen for?' which points to the present, the now, and opens up the realm of purpose and meaning. This is the question which we should ask all through our lives, as our relative rounding is never completed and individuation never ends, though analysis as a treatment does.

There are many different ways which lead to fulfilment and wholeness. Everyone has to find his or her own path. The two I have written about here are those I know best because they are mine, in fact they are an expression of what I am. I am well aware that searching for one's own truth can be a long journey, wearying at times and at others exhilarating, filling one with joy. We all have a centre of gravity within us; the way we take to discover it is nobody's concern but our own, and the only thing that matters is to go on looking until we catch a glimmer of where the treasure is. Whether we reach it or not is uncertain; it seems as if the search is more important than the goal.

EPILOGUE

I have quite often been asked how I can be a Jungian analyst and at the same time a member of the Roman Catholic Church. From a purely intellectual point of view there is no answer to this question. On the one hand theologians can point to this or that concept which does not seem to square with one of theirs; on the other, psychologists may be at a loss to see how a religious outlook can be reconciled with an analytical one. For me the answer is relatively simple: in Jungian terms I am not a thinking type, I apprehend and comprehend from a centre other than mind. In my own language I would say that Jung's approach and attitude to man in the universe has enriched my faith and kept any doubts I may have healthily in consciousness. Conversely my faith has illuminated many of Jung's ideas and helped me to understand what he was trying to do and what he hoped to achieve on his way to experience and greater awareness.

The descent into our underworld is always dangerous, because of the power of the shades of the past to seduce us into staying with them. We may also be enticed by visions of the future, 'Mine eyes have seen the glory of the coming of the Lord'. Both the past and the future live within us and are parts of our life; they are a fundamental pair of opposites which we have to come to terms with. I have become very conscious of past joy and pain, and of fear and hope for the future in myself. I know that every day at every moment of the day these two have to be united in me, into the now of my life, into my present which is above time.

BIBLIOGRAPHY

Gerhard Adler : *The Living Symbol*, Routledge, 1961
M. A. Atwood : *Hermetic Philosophy and Alchemy*, Julian Press, 1960.
P. Teilhard de Chardin : *The Phenomenon of Man*, Fontana, 1951
A. Eddington : *The Nature of the Physical World*, Everyman Library (Dent), 1935
R. D. Gray : *Goethe the Alchemist*, C.U.P., 1967
F. C. Happold : *Religious Faith and Twentieth Century Man*, Penguin, 1969
R. Hobson : Loneliness, *Journal of Analytical Psychology*, Jan 1974
E. J. Homyard : *Alchemy*, Penguin, 1957
C. G. Jung : *Collected Works* :
    Vol. 5 : *Symbols of Transformation*, Routledge, 2nd Ed., 1967
    Vol. 9 : Part 1 : *Archetypes and the Collective Unconscious* 2nd Ed., Routledge, 1969
    Part 2 : *Aion*, 1959
    Vol. 10 : *Civilisation in Transition*, Routledge, 3rd Ed., 1973
    Vol. 11 : *Psychology and Religion*, Routledge, 3rd Ed., 1970
    Vol. 12 : *Psychology and Religion*, Routledge, 2nd Ed., 1969
    Vol. 14 : *Mysterium Coniunctionis*, Routledge, 1963
    Vol. 16 : *The Practice of Psychotherapy* Routledge, 1954
Memories, Dreams and Reflections, Fontana, 1967
C. G. Jung Letters, 1906–1950, Routledge, 1973

The Sacred Congregation for Divine Worship : *Penance: Introduction to the New Rite*, Catholic Truth Society, 1974
Jeremy Seabrook : *Loneliness,* M. T. Smith and New Society, 1973
Gersham Scholem : *Major Trends in Jewish Mysticism,* Allen and Unwin, 1971
Holmes Welch : *The Parting of the Way,* Beacon Press, 1966
Heinrich Zimmer : *Philosophies of India,* Routledge, 1951